Learning with the Sunday Gospels

TAKE-HOME SHEETS

Part Two:
Trinity Sunday to Christ the King

These worksheets accompany the book:

Learning with the Sunday Gospels
Volume Two:
Trinity Sunday to Christ the King

Also available:

Learning with the Sunday Gospels Volume One:
Advent to Pentecost

Learning with the Sunday Gospels Take-home Sheets
Part One: Advent to Pentecost

Learning with the Sunday Gospels

TAKE-HOME SHEETS

Part Two:
Trinity Sunday to Christ the King

Leslie J. Francis and Diane Drayson

MOWBRAY

Mowbray
A Continuum imprint
Wellington House, 125 Strand, London WC2R 0BB
370 Lexington Avenue, New York, NY 10017-6550

First published 2000

British Library Cataloguing-in-Publication Data
A catalogue record for this book is available from the British Library.

ISBN 0-264-67498-7

Printed and bound in Great Britain by Martin's the Printers Ltd, Berwick upon Tweed.

CONTENTS

Preface
Introduction

Preface

The Revised Common Lectionary is bringing many of the churches closer together as they share and reflect on common passages of Scripture Sunday by Sunday. One of the strengths of this lectionary is the way in which the distinctive voices of the three synoptic gospels are heard in the year of Matthew, the year of Mark and the year of Luke. The aim of *Learning with the Sunday Gospels* is to make sure that the children of the church are introduced to these gospels alongside the adult worshippers.

As in our earlier programmes for children, the present programme reflects two deeply held personal commitments: commitment to parish ministry and commitment to good quality educational theory and practice.

We are grateful to those congregations with whom we have worked and worshipped for their part in shaping our thinking and practice. We also wish to express our appreciation to the Principal and Governors of Trinity College Carmarthen for fostering and encouraging our work; to Ruth McCurry for commissioning and helping to structure the project; to the Revd Enid Morgan for proposing a Welsh translation of our work; to the Revd Robert Paterson for helping us steer a path through the lectionary; to Bee Evans, Johnnie Gray, Rachel Grovenor and Ellie Nixon from SS Mary and John School who read and tested the activities; and to Anne Rees for shaping the manuscript.

Leslie J. Francis
Diane Drayson

Welsh National Centre for Religious Education
University of Wales, Bangor
September 1999

Introduction

*L*earning with the Sunday Gospels is a project-based programme of Christian education. It is organized around the gospel readings proposed by the Revised Common Lectionary as adopted by the Church of England and the Church of Wales. The programme is sufficiently flexible to suit the many other churches which are following the same basic lectionary. Its purpose is to develop understanding of biblical themes and to promote a positive attitude towards worship.

This volume provides photocopiable take-home sheets to support the churches' work with children. These sheets continue the learning activities at home and communicate to parents the content of the sessions.

Two different types of sheet are included for each session. The two sheets can be photocopied back-to-back or used separately. It may be appropriate to enlarge some activities to A3 as they are copied.

One sheet comprises the following sections:

- **Today at church**, which gives a brief explanation of how the theme links to the gospel or the church's year;
- **Gospel theme**, which identifies the main theme of the gospel passage read in church;
- **Gospel passage**, which reproduces the key verses from the gospel reading;
- **Prayer**, which provides a brief collect specially written to reflect the gospel theme;
- **Talking points**, which are designed to help those at home talk with the children about their learning;
- **Activity for younger children**, which offers suggestions on project activities to explore the theme with younger children.

The other sheet comprises activities which explore the theme of the Sunday gospel. These activities have been designed with 7 to 11-year-olds in mind but the children either side of this age range might find them enjoyable as well. They can be undertaken by children on their own or can be shared with adults and other children at home.

Choose for yourself how to use these take-home sheets, according to the needs of your group.

In churches where children's groups are run on Sunday morning alongside the main service, children will generally take the sheets home after the service. They should be encouraged to show these sheets to their parents and to use the Bible passage and the prayer throughout the week.

In churches where children's groups are run on a weekday, the children will generally take the sheets home after the weekday session but they may be invited to bring their project work back to the service on Sunday. The prayer can then be used in the Sunday service.

Churches which explore the same theme over several weeks, for example in readiness for a monthly family service, may decide to send the sheets home with the children halfway through the sessions and invite the children to bring their project work back in time for the last session before the service. A display of their work from the take-home sheets can then be shown at the service.

Make a waterfall

You will need

plastic bottle
bricks or boxes
water

stones or pebbles
plants

What to do

1.   If you have a garden, ask a parent or guardian if you can use a small part of it to make a waterfall.

2.   In a waterfall, water needs to fall from a height. Find a part of the garden that has high and low parts, or build a cliff at least 30 cm high from bricks or wooden blocks. Cover the top with soil and place stones or pebbles around the edge for water to trickle through.

3.   Put more stones or pebbles at the bottom of the cliff and add some small plants.

4.   Cut a small hole towards the bottom of a plastic bottle (such as a lemonade bottle). Whenever you want to enjoy the waterfall, fill the bottle with water and place it at the top of the cliff so that the water trickles out the bottle, over the stones and down the cliff. Vary the flow of water by changing the size of the hole in the bottle. Fill up the bottle as it empties.

5.   If you do not have a garden, make a waterfall inside the house by decorating a plastic bowl and sitting the bottle on something like a saucepan inside the bowl.

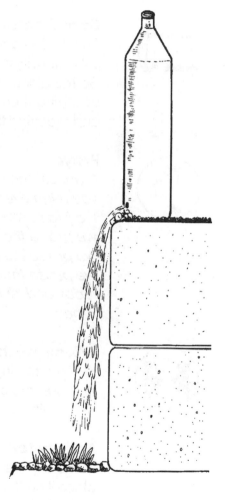

The waterfall offers a feeling of mystery.
On Trinity Sunday we celebrate the mystery of God.

This belongs to: . . . .

Waterfall

Today at church
Today at church we talked about the feeling of mystery when watching a waterfall. Then we celebrated the mystery of God as Father, Son and Holy Spirit. Today is the feast of the Holy Trinity.

Gospel theme
The doctrine of the Trinity affirms that God has been made known in the world in three characteristic ways, as Father, as Son, and as Holy Spirit. The doctrine of the Trinity is rooted in Matthew's account of Jesus' command to the disciples to baptise in 'the name of the Father and of the Son and of the Holy Spirit'.

Gospel passage (Matthew 28.18-20)
And Jesus came and said to the disciples,
'All authority in heaven and on earth has been given to me.
Go therefore and make disciples of all nations,
baptizing them in the name of the Father and of the Son and of the Holy Spirit,
and teaching them to obey everything that I have commanded you.'

Prayer
Glorious and Holy Trinity,
you reign over all things.
We praise the Father,
we praise the Son,
we praise the Holy Spirit,
we praise the Glorious and Holy Trinity;
today and always.
Amen.

Talking points
❖ our feeling of mystery watching a waterfall;
❖ our response of awe and wonder watching a waterfall;
❖ Trinity Sunday celebrates the mystery of God.

Activity for younger children
Make a waterfall. Fill a plastic bottle (such as a lemonade bottle) with water and place it on the side of the bath so that the water runs out and down the inside edge of the bath.

This belongs to: . . . .

Design a night sky

You will need

glow-in-the-dark star stickers or paint   paper
pencil   Blu-tack or masking tape

What to do

1. Copy a star constellation onto a large sheet of paper. Make the picture large but keep the position and shape of the stars as correct as you can.
2. Ask a parent or guardian if you can make a night sky picture directly on a wall or ceiling or if you need to make it on poster paper to attach to the wall.
3. If you are making the picture directly on the wall or ceiling, attach your constellation picture in place with Blue-tack or masking tape. Use a pencil to make a small hole through the paper to show the position of each star. This will leave a small pencil mark. Remove the paper and place a glow-in-the-dark star on each mark, or paint a small circle on each mark with glow-in-the-dark paint. (You do not have to paint a star shape.) Use stars or circles of different sizes to give a three-dimensional effect.
4. If you are making a poster to hang on the wall, then place a sticker or paint a circle over each star position on your paper.

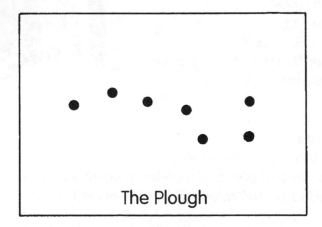

The Plough

**The night sky offers a feeling of mystery.
On Trinity Sunday we celebrate the mystery of God.**

This belongs to: . . . .

Night sky

Today at church
Today at church we talked about the feeling of mystery when watching the night sky. Then we celebrated the mystery of God as Father, Son and Holy Spirit. Today is the feast of the Holy Trinity.

Gospel theme
The doctrine of the Trinity affirms that God has been made known in the world in three characteristic ways, as Father, as Son, and as Holy Spirit. In John's gospel Jesus' conversation with Nicodemus provides biblical roots for the distinctive activities of God as Father, Jesus as Son, and the Holy Spirit.

Gospel passage (John 3.1–3)
There was a Pharisee named Nicodemus,
a leader of the Jews.
He came to Jesus by night
and said to him,
'Rabbi, we know that you are a teacher who has come from God;
for no one can do these signs that you do apart from the presence of God.'
Jesus answered him,
'Very truly, I tell you, no one can see the kingdom of God
without being born from above.'

Prayer
Holy, holy, holy
is the Lord of sky and sea.
Praise to the Father,
praise to the Son,
praise to the Holy Spirit,
praise to the Glorious and Holy Trinity;
now and for ever.
Amen.

Talking points
❖ our feeling of mystery experiencing the night sky;
❖ our response of awe and wonder at the night sky;
❖ Trinity Sunday celebrates the mystery of God.

Activity for younger children
Make a poster of the night sky. Use bright paint or cut out paper shapes to glue onto black paper. Display the poster in your bedroom.

This belongs to: . . . .

Make a rocket game

You will need

paper or card   scissors
pens or pencils   straws
large sheet of paper

What to do

1. Make rocket shapes from paper or light card. Experiment to see what type of paper and size of rocket is best for the game.
2. To play a game with a friend, each put a rocket at one end of the large sheet of paper. Use a straw each to blow your rocket towards the other end of the paper. The rules are:
   ★ The straw must not touch the rocket.
   ★ The first rocket over the finishing line is the winner.
   ★ If a rocket is blown off the side of the paper it must return to the start.
3. To play a game by yourself, design a course for your rocket by drawing stars on a large sheet of paper. Blow through a straw to direct the rocket from star to star.

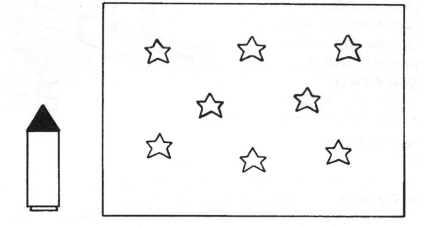

Space travel offers a feeling of mystery.
On Trinity Sunday we celebrate the mystery of God.

This belongs to: . . . .

Space travel

Today at church

Today at church we talked about the vastness and mystery of space. Then we celebrated the mystery of God as Father, Son and Holy Spirit. Today is the feast of the Holy Trinity.

Gospel theme

The doctrine of the Trinity affirms that God has been made known in the world in three characteristic ways, as Father, as Son, and as Holy Spirit. In John's gospel Jesus' farewell discourse to his disciples before the arrest and trial provides biblical roots for the distinctive activities of God as Father, Jesus as Son, and the Holy Spirit.

Gospel passage (John 16.13-15)

Jesus said, 'When the Spirit of truth comes,
he will guide you into all the truth;
for he will not speak on his own,
but will speak whatever he hears,
and he will declare to you the things that are to come.
He will glorify me,
because he will take what is mine and declare it to you.
All that the Father has is mine.
For this reason I said
that he will take what is mine and declare it to you.'

Prayer

Holy and Glorious Trinity,
you are older than time
and greater than space.
We praise the Father,
we praise the Son,
we praise the Holy Spirit,
we praise the Holy and Glorious Trinity;
today and always.
Amen.

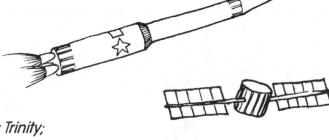

Talking points

* ❖ our ideas about the vastness and mystery of space;
* ❖ our response of awe and wonder at the mystery of space;
* ❖ Trinity Sunday celebrates the mystery of God.

Activity for younger children

Design a rocket from cardboard boxes and tubes and from plastic cartons. Take it outside to see how high you can launch it.

This belongs to: . . . .

Experiment with foundations

You will need

Lego or construction material   soil

What to do

1. Build two small identical model houses. Change one house by adding foundations to the bottom of it.

2. Use the garden or a pot of soil for an experiment to see how foundations keep a house in place. Place one house so that the foundations are buried in the soil. Press the soil firmly in place around the foundations. Place the second house on top of the soil.

3. Experiment to see the difference that the foundations make. Throw a soft ball or blow through a straw or suck with a vacuum cleaner or squirt with a hose or try in any other way to make the houses move or collapse. Which house is stronger?

4. In the weeks and months ahead, look closely at any building sites you pass in order to see the types of foundations they use and how deep the foundations are.

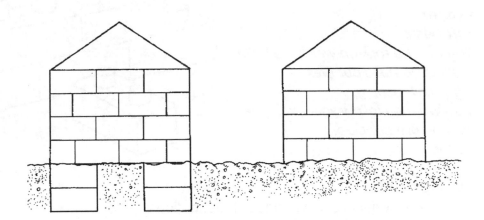

**Houses need firm foundations.
Jesus' teaching is a firm foundation for our lives.**

This belongs to: . . . .

Foundations

Today at church
Today at church we talked about foundations. Then we listened to Jesus' story about the wise man who built his house on rock.

Gospel theme
The sermon on the mount ends with the well known picture contrasting those who build their lives on the words of Jesus and those who do not. The contrast is like that between those who build houses on rock and those who build houses on sand.

Gospel passage (Matthew 7.24-27)
Jesus said, 'Everyone then who hears these words of mine and acts on them
will be like a wise man who built his house on rock.
The rain fell, the floods came,
and the winds blew and beat on that house,
but it did not fall,
because it had been founded on rock.
And everyone who hears these words of mine
and does not act on them
will be like a foolish man who built his house on sand.
The rain fell, and the floods came,
and the winds blew and beat against that house,
and it fell –
and great was its fall!'

Prayer
Lord Jesus,
you are the rock on which we build.
Help us to build our lives
on your teaching,
that we may follow your example;
for you are our God.
Amen.

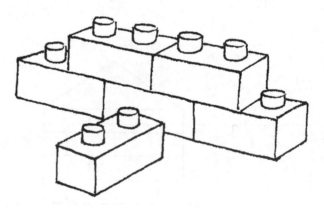

Talking points
❖ our experiences and images of foundations;
❖ the Christian way of life built on foundations;
❖ Jesus calls us to act on his teaching.

Activity for younger children
Build towers from boxes or blocks. Build one with a small base or foundation and another with a large base or foundation. Which is stronger?

This belongs to: . . . .

Keep a diary

Is Sunday the same as any other day of the week or is it special?
Keep a diary of your activities for a week and see if there are special things that you do or don't do on Sunday.

Monday
Tuesday
Wednesday
Thursday
Friday
Saturday
Sunday

God planned Sunday for our benefit.
Sunday is a special day.

This belongs to: . . . .

Sundays

Today at church
Today at church we talked about how Sunday can be kept as a special day. Then we listened to how Jesus thought about the Jewish Sabbath.

Gospel theme
In Mark's gospel, Jesus is seen to break the sabbath law in two ways, by encouraging his disciples to pluck heads of grain and by healing the man who had the withered hand. Jesus' reply that 'the sabbath was made for humankind and not humankind for the sabbath' stands at the heart of the debate concerning the Christian attitude to keeping Sunday special.

Gospel passage (Mark 3.1–4)
Again Jesus entered the synagogue,
and a man was there who had a withered hand.
They watched him to see whether he would cure him on the sabbath,
so that they might accuse him.
And he said to the man who had the withered hand,
'Come forward.'
Then he said to them,
'Is it lawful to do good or to do harm on the sabbath,
to save life or to kill?'
But they were silent.

Prayer
Lord Jesus Christ,
you made Sunday special
by rising from the dead.
Help us to give you special place
in the Sundays throughout our lives,
that others may see the power of your resurrection;
for you are our God.
Amen.

Talking points
❖   our experiences of Sunday;
❖   Jesus' attitude to the sabbath;
❖   our response to keeping Sundays special.

Activity for younger children
Sunday is a special day. Plan a special activity for each Sunday. It could be a scrap book that you draw in only on Sundays. Draw and write about the Bible story for the week or about the best thing that has happened all week.

This belongs to: . . . .

Make a Roman centurion's shield

You will need

cardboard   cooking foil

red paper   scissors

glue   pens or pencils

sticky tape

What to do

1. A Roman shield was curved. Roll up the cardboard and keep it in a roll for a few minutes until it is ready to keep a curved shape.
2. Cut out a shield shape from the curved cardboard.
3. Cover the shield with cooking foil or paint it with grey or metallic paint.
4. Cut the Roman eagle design from red paper and glue it to the centre of the shield.
5. Tape a cardboard handle to the back so you can hold it.

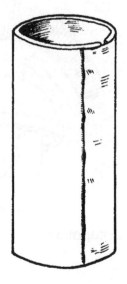 

> **The Roman centurion was a stranger in Israel.**
> **Jesus welcomed him for his faith.**

This belongs to: . . . .

Roman centurion

Today at church
Today at church we talked about Roman centurions. Then we heard how Jesus accepted the faith of a centurion at Capernaum and healed his slave.

Gospel theme
The Roman centurion is an important figure in Luke's gospel for three reasons. Clearly the centurion represented the Gentile world. The centurion was in Capernaum as part of a foreign army of occupation. Although a foreigner, the centurion was sympathetic, and not antagonistic, to Judaism. Jesus said to the centurion, 'Not even in Israel have I found such faith.'

Gospel passage (Luke 7.6-7, 9-10)
When Jesus was not far from the house,
the centurion sent friends to say to him,
'Lord, do not trouble yourself,
for I am not worthy to have you come under my roof;
therefore I did not presume to come to you.
But only speak the word, and let my servant be healed.
When Jesus heard this he was amazed at him,
and turning to the crowd that followed him, he said,
'I tell you, not even in Israel have I found such faith.'
When those who had been sent returned to the house,
they found the slave in good health.

Prayer
Lord Jesus Christ,
you accepted the faith of the Roman centurion.
Give us faith like his,
that we too may know your power;
for you are our God.
Amen.

Talking points
❖ our images of the Roman centurion;
❖ the centurion as a Gentile in a foreign army of occupation;
❖ Jesus' acceptance of the centurion's faith.

Activity for younger children
Roman soldiers and centurions marched long distances. Ask an older brother or sister or an adult to teach you how to march. March around the house and yard several times, pretending to be a Roman centurion.

This belongs to: . . . .

Gather a repair box

Think

- How often do you need to repair something?
- Can you easily find the repair tools you need when you want them?
- Would it be easier to keep a special box full of tools?

What to do

1. Find a sturdy box or carrier to contain tools.
2. Talk to members of your family about the type of repairs they often need to do and what tools they would find useful. This could include tape, stapler and staples, string, hammer, nails, screwdriver, needle, thread and scissors.
3. Collect as many of these tools as you can and stack them neatly in the box. Find a convenient place in the house to store the repair box, a place where everyone will be able to find it quickly.

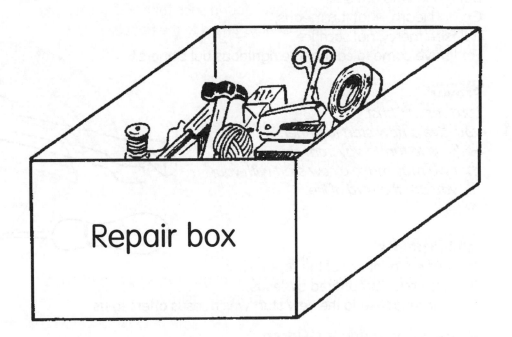

Repair box

**Repaired toys are given a new start.
Jesus offers us a new start.**

This belongs to: . . . .

Repair shop

Today at church
Today at church we talked about different kinds of repair shops where things are mended and given a new start. Then we heard how Jesus offers us a new start.

Gospel theme
A key theme of the gospels is that Jesus holds out to people a new start. Jesus heals those who are hurt and welcomes those who are alienated. Jesus calls Matthew from his work as someone who collected taxes from the Jewish people on behalf of the Roman authorities. Jesus welcomes sinners to eat with him.

Gospel passage (Matthew 9.10-13)
And as Jesus sat at dinner in the house,
many tax-collectors and sinners came
and were sitting with him and his disciples.
When the Pharisees saw this,
they said to his disciples,
'Why does your teacher eat with tax-collectors and sinners?'
But when he heard this, he said,
'Those who are well have no need of a physician,
but those who are sick.
Go and learn what this means,
"I desire mercy, not sacrifice."
For I have come to call not the righteous but sinners.'

Prayer
Lord Jesus Christ,
you give a new start to sinners.
Help us to turn away from sin,
that we may make a new start with you;
for you are the Lord of life.
Amen.

Talking points
❖ our experiences of the repair shop;
❖ the new start offered by Jesus;
❖ our response to the new start which Jesus offers to us.

Activity for younger children
Collect any toys and books that are broken. Decide which ones need to be thrown away and which ones can be repaired and given a new start.

This belongs to: . . . .

Make saltdough sculptures

You will need

1 cup salt

1 cup water

paint

3 cups flour

a dribble of cooking oil

PVA glue

What to do

1. Make the saltdough by mixing all the ingredients together. If it is too dry, add more water.

2. Knead or push the dough for at least two minutes. Leave it for half an hour before using it. (Any dough not used within a day needs to be thrown out.)

3. Use the dough to make two sculptures of hands, one of hands in conflict (perhaps fists smashing together) and one of hands at peace (perhaps shaking or holding hands).

4. Ask an adult to cook the sculptures for you. Small sculptures need to be cooked for an hour at 150°C or 300°F or gas mark 2. Large sculptures need to be cooked for 3 hours at 100°C or 225°F or gas mark 1. Cook them until they are thoroughly dry. Test them by tapping them on the bottom. If they sound hollow, they are ready.

5. Paint the sculptures and varnish them with PVA (white) glue.

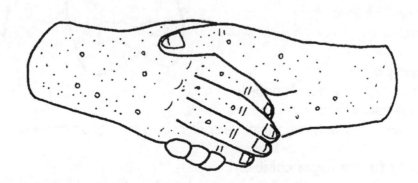

**Hands can show conflict or peace.
Jesus was caught in the conflict between good
and evil.**

This belongs to: . . . .

Conflict

Today at church
Today at church we talked about conflict. Then we heard how Jesus was caught in the conflict between good and evil.

Gospel theme
Right from the beginning of his gospel Mark contrasts the way in which the sick, the possessed and the outcasts flock to Jesus with the way in which the religious leaders refused to recognise Jesus' authority and stirred up controversy against him. Even Jesus' closest family questioned his sanity, while the scribes insisted on attributing Jesus' actions to evil sources.

Gospel passage (Mark 3.20-22)
The crowd came together again,
so that Jesus and his companions could not even eat.
When Jesus' family heard it, they went out to restrain him,
for people were saying, 'He has gone out of his mind.'
And the scribes who came down from Jerusalem said,
'He has Beelzebul,
and by the ruler of the demons he casts out demons.'

Prayer
Lord Jesus Christ,
you faced conflict in your ministry.
When we face conflict,
help us to follow your example,
that we may choose the right way
and not the wrong way;
now and always.
Amen.

Talking points
❖   our experiences of conflict;
❖   the conflict between good and evil;
❖   how Jesus was caught in the conflict between good and evil.

Activity for younger children
Do some hand painting. Cover your hands with paint. Print them on a sheet of paper, trying to show hands in conflict or hands fighting. Cover your hands with a different colour paint and print them to show hands in peace.

This belongs to: . . . .

Make a twist-out teardrop

You will need

thin coloured card   pencil
craft knife

What to do

1. Draw a teardrop shape on the cardboard in the shape you want. Lightly draw two pencil lines making a cross through the centre. Remember never to cut along these lines.
2. Draw in lines following the pattern below. Cut along these lines with a craft knife.
3. Gently twist the outer circle away from the centre.
4. Starting at the rim, form the first twist by gently turning the central section at a right angle to the outer ring.
5. Continue to form the twists by turning each ring at the same angle, moving towards the centre until all sections have been twisted.
6. Hang your tear twist in your room. When you feel sad, remember that Jesus cares about our sorrow.

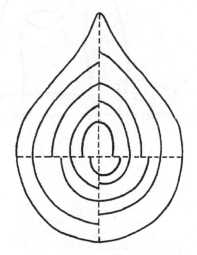
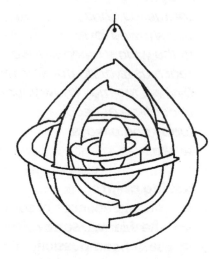

Tears are a sign of sorrow.
Jesus cares about our sorrow.

This belongs to: . . . .

Tears

Today at church
Today at church we talked about how tears show our sorrow and pain. Then we heard how Jesus responded to the tears of the widow at Nain.

Gospel theme
Jesus' encounter with the widow at Nain shows his compassion and power. His heart goes out to the mother of the dead man. Her loss and her desolation were profound. Already a widow, now she had lost her only son. Jesus' message to her is simple and direct. 'Do not weep', he said.

Gospel passage (Luke 7.12–14)
As Jesus approached the gate of the town,
a man who had died was being carried out.
He was his mother's only son,
and she was a widow;
and with her was a large crowd from the town.
When the Lord saw her,
he had compassion for her and said to her,
'Do not weep.'
Then he came forward and touched the bier,
and the bearers stood still.
And he said, 'Young man, I say to you, rise!'

Prayer
Lord Jesus Christ,
you showed love
to the widow when she was sad.
Teach us to bring our sorrows to you,
that we too may know your love
in our time of need;
today and always.
Amen.

Talking points
❖   our experiences of sorrow and tears;
❖   the widow's sorrow;
❖   Jesus' compassion.

Activity for younger children
Make a teardrop bracelet. Cut teardrop shapes from clear plastic. Punch a hole in the top of each. Thread them onto wool or coloured string, knotting each teardrop in place. Use your bracelet to remind yourself that Jesus cares when we are sad.

This belongs to: . . . .

Make a 'friends' photoframe

You will need

corrugated cardboard	ruler
pencil	craft knife
wallpaper paste	newspaper
string	paint
PVA glue or varnish	

What to do

1. Trace the shape and size of a photograph onto the corrugated cardboard. Draw a frame around this, about 5 cm larger than the photograph. Cut out the frame. (Keep the central piece for the backing.)

2. Paint both pieces with a good coat of wallpaper paste and leave them to dry. (This will make sure the frame does not buckle.)

3. Tear newspaper into short strips. Dip them in the wallpaper paste and wrap them around the frame to cover it completely, front and back. Allow it to dry and then add a second layer.

4. Glue the backing board to the back of the frame, leaving the top open so that you can slip in a photograph.

5. Decorate the frame with pieces of newspaper folded into bows or shaped into crescent moons and glued on, or dip short lengths of string in glue and arrange these on the frame.

6. Paint the frame then coat it with varnish or PVA glue. When dry, put inside it a photograph of a friend, or add your own photograph and give it to a friend.

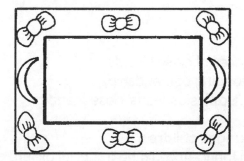

**We enjoy having close friends.
The twelve disciples were Jesus' close friends.**

This belongs to: . . . .

Friends

Today at church
Today at church we talked about friends. Then we learnt about the names of Jesus' close friends, the twelve apostles.

Gospel theme
The synoptic gospels show Jesus as working closely with a group of twelve special disciples. The number of special disciples reflects the twelve tribes of Israel and so foreshadows the new Israel founded by Jesus.

Gospel passage (Matthew 10.1–4)
Then Jesus summoned his twelve disciples
and gave them authority over unclean spirits,
to cast them out,
and to cure every disease and every sickness.
These are the names of the twelve apostles:
first, Simon, also known as Peter, and his brother Andrew;
James son of Zebedee, and his brother John;
Philip and Bartholomew;
Thomas and Matthew the tax-collector;
James son of Alphaeus, and Thaddaeus;
Simon the Cananaean, and Judas Iscariot,
the one who betrayed him.

Prayer
Lord Jesus Christ,
you chose twelve disciples
to be your close followers.
Call us to follow in their footsteps,
that we may share their closeness to you;
for you are our God.
Amen.

Talking points
* ❖ our experiences of close friends;
* ❖ our understanding of friendship;
* ❖ the twelve disciples as Jesus' close friends.

Activity for younger children
Make a gift for a friend. It could be a special picture or model, or you could help an adult to cook a gift. Wrap the present and give it away.

This belongs to: . . . .

Make a growth chart

You will need

plain cardboard   sticky tape
ruler   pencils or pens

What to do

1. Make a growth chart to keep, and record on it different stages of your growth.

2. Tape together as many sheets of cardboard (postcards or cereal packets or art card) as you need to make a strip that is at least 20 cm taller than you are.

3. Attach it to a wall or cupboard, then measure from the floor to mark the chart in centimetres. (If you hang it up first, then it will not matter if it does not rest on the floor. Your measurements will still be correct.)

4. Measure yourself and mark this height with the date. Draw a decorative vine or plant growing up towards this height.

5. Every few months measure yourself again and mark the new height and date. Next to these heights you can also write new achievements, such as advanced computer levels or running speed or reading progress. Keep drawing the vine or plant towards each new height.

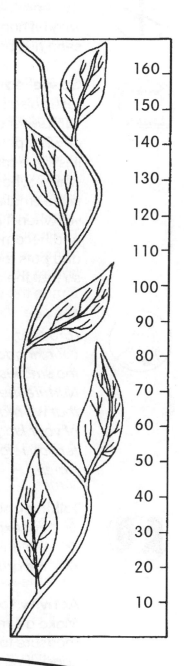

**We grow in many ways.
The kingdom of God keeps growing.**

This belongs to: . . . .

Growing up

Today at church
Today at church we talked about growing up. Then we listened to Jesus' story about the great shrub growing from the small mustard seed.

Gospel theme
The parable of the mustard seed demonstrates the natural processes of growth without human intervention. The point is that the kingdom of God is like that too. The seed has been planted and nothing can stop the growth.

Gospel passage (Mark 4.30-32)
Jesus also said,
'With what can we compare the kingdom of God,
or what parable will we use for it?
It is like a mustard seed,
which, when sown upon the ground,
is the smallest of all the seeds on earth;
yet when it is sown it grows up
and becomes the greatest of all shrubs,
and puts forth large branches,
so that the birds of the air can make nests in its shade.'

Prayer
Lord God,
your kingdom grows from
the smallest seeds.
Nurture the seeds of your love in our hearts,
that we may grow in the ways
of your kingdom;
for you reign as king for ever.
Amen.

Talking points
❖ our experiences of growing up;
❖ the natural processes of growth;
❖ the growth of the kingdom of God.

Activity for younger children
Make a simple growth chart. Decorate a long sheet of paper or card. Glue a tape measure to the edge and attach it to the wall. Mark your height and the date on the chart. Every few months measure your height to see if you have grown.

This belongs to: . . . .

Keep a forgiveness chart

How often are you forgiven? How often do you forgive others? Forgiveness can be as simple as saying 'I'm sorry' or it can mean making up after a fight. Keep a record of this week in the chart below. In one colour fill in all the times you have been forgiven. In a different colour fill in all the times you have forgiven others.

Monday	Tuesday
Wednesday	**Thursday**
Friday	**Saturday**
Sunday	

**Forgiveness is important in our daily lives.
Jesus offers us forgiveness.**

This belongs to: . . . .

Feeling forgiven

Today at church
Today at church we talked about feeling forgiveness. Then we heard Jesus' story about how someone forgave two debts - a large debt and a small debt.

Gospel theme
The theme of forgiveness and of rehabilitation is at the very heart of the Christian gospel. The parable of the two debtors illustrates the theme of forgiveness by drawing on the image of debts cancelled and the gratitude that follows.

Gospel passage (Luke 7.41–43)
Jesus said, 'A certain creditor had two debtors;
one owed five hundred denarii, and the other fifty.
When they could not pay,
he cancelled the debts for both of them.
Now which of them will love him more?'
Simon answered,
'I suppose the one for whom he cancelled the greater debt.'

Prayer
Lord Jesus Christ,
you forgive those
who turn to you for mercy.
Turn our hearts to receive your forgiveness,
that we may forgive those who do wrong against us;
for you are the God of mercy.
Amen.

Talking points
❖ our experiences of being forgiven;
❖ forgiveness in the gospel;
❖ accepting the forgiveness which Jesus offers to us.

Activity for younger children
Make a 'sorry' chart. Each time you hear someone say the word 'sorry', tick the chart. Each time you remember to say 'sorry', tick the chart or draw in a smiley face. Being forgiven and forgiving others is important.

This belongs to: . . . .

Make a pet

If you do not already have a pet in your house, then make one of your own. Here are two ideas.

Pet rock

1.   Find a smooth stone or rock with interesting colours.
2.   Wash it and scrub it to remove all the dirt. Polish it with a soft cloth.
3.   If you want a shiny surface, varnish it or coat it with PVA glue.
4.   Prepare a suitable habitat for your pet rock, such as a sand tray with smaller pebbles for company.

Pet crawler

1.   Cut out a long oval from sheepskin or a thick material.
2.   Glue on eyes (black felt or fabric) and a long red tongue.
3.   Place the crawler on your clothing and gently stroke it to make it curl and crawl along.

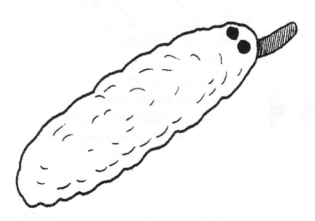

Pets need love and care.
God cares for us.

This belongs to: . . . .

Pets

Today at church

Today at church we talked about how we care for our pets. Then we heard about the care which God shows for us.

Gospel theme

After Jesus commissions the twelve apostles to go out on their first mission, Matthew presents a collection of teaching to equip them for that work. God cares about them and will take care of them. Their God cares for the sparrows and they are of more value than many sparrows.

Gospel passage (Matthew 10.29-31)

Jesus said, 'Are not two sparrows sold for a penny?
Yet not one of them will fall to the ground
unperceived by your Father.
And even the hairs of your head are all counted.
So do not be afraid;
you are of more value than many sparrows.'

Prayer

Lord Jesus Christ,
you show care for all birds and beasts.
Help us to share your concern
for all living creatures,
that we too may know
your care for us;
now and always.
Amen.

Talking points

❖   our care for our pets;
❖   the commitment such care shows;
❖   accepting the care which God shows for us.

Activity for younger children

Make a pet crawler. Cut out a long oval from sheepskin or thick fabric. Glue on fabric eyes and a long red tongue. Place the crawler on your sleeve and stroke it gently to make it curl and crawl up your arm.

This belongs to: . . . .

Make a 'peace globe'

You will need

balloon   newspaper
flour and water paste   scissors
ribbon   paint or coloured paper

What to do

1.   Blow up the balloon and fasten it tightly.
2.   With the help of an adult, make flour and water paste. Heat 1 cup of flour and 3 cups of water in a saucepan, stirring until it thickens. Leave it to cool.
3.   Tear up pieces of newspaper, soak them in the paste and put them on the balloon. You will need about five layers of paper. (If you do not want to paint the globe, the last layer should be coloured paper.) Place it on a plastic bag and leave it for about two days to dry thoroughly.
4.   Paint the globe. Add hand shapes cut out of coloured paper, or hand prints in different colours of paint. Arrange them to look like hands meeting around the world in peace.
5.   Cut two small holes in the top of the globe to thread ribbon through. Hang the globe in your room.

**Our hands can meet others in peace.
Jesus offers us peace.**

This belongs to: . . . .

Speaking with hands

Today at church
Today at church we talked about how people use their hands to say 'peace' to each other in the communion service. Then we heard how Jesus brought peace to the storm.

Gospel theme
The opening chapters of Mark's gospel portray Jesus as one who has authority over the powers of evil. The storm represents evil and chaos. Jesus says to the storm 'Peace! Be still.' Peace is that context in which God's will for the creation is realised.

Gospel passage (Mark 4.37–39)
A great gale arose, and the waves beat into the boat,
so that the boat was already being swamped.
But he was in the stern, asleep on the cushion;
and they woke him up and said to him,
'Teacher, do you not care that we are perishing?'
He woke up and rebuked the wind, and said to the sea,
'Peace! Be still!'
Then the wind ceased, and there was a dead calm.

Prayer
Lord Jesus Christ,
you brought peace to the storm.
Teach us to turn to you
when our lives are stormy and rough,
that we may hear your words of peace
and experience your calm in our hearts;
today and every day.
Amen.

Talking points
❖ our experiences of expression through hands;
❖ the symbolism of the Peace;
❖ the peace which Jesus offers.

Activity for younger children
Make a card to wish peace to a friend. Use your hands as a sign of peace. Paint over the inside of your hands, each hand in a different colour. Make two handprints on the front of the card by placing your hands down, one after the other.

This belongs to: . . . .

Make a model television

You will need

large cardboard box   pencil
scissors or craft knife

What to do

1.   Choose a cardboard box which is larger than your head and shoulders.
2.   Cut off the top flaps.
3.   On the bottom, draw a rounded frame about 5 cm in from the edges. Cut it out. This is the television screen.
4.   Draw or glue on control buttons.
5.   Write your own news script about home, school or church news. Sit behind your model television to 'broadcast' your news to family and friends.

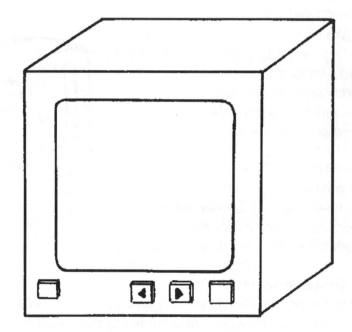

**Televisions broadcast the news of the world.
The best news is how much Jesus has done for us.**

This belongs to: . . . .

Television news

Today at church
Today at church we talked about how the news on the television gets things known quickly. Then we heard how Jesus told Legion to make known how much God had done for him.

Gospel theme
The healing of Legion once again demonstrates Jesus' power over the forces of evil. Such clear evidence of Jesus' power over evil deserved broadcasting. The healed man went away proclaiming throughout the city how much Jesus had done for him.

Gospel passage (Luke 8.38–39)
The man from whom the demons had gone begged that he might be with him; but Jesus sent him away, saying, 'Return to your home, and declare how much God has done for you.' So he went away, proclaiming throughout the city how much Jesus had done for him.

Prayer
Lord Jesus Christ,
you told Legion
to proclaim your healing power to the world.
Help us to proclaim
all you have done in our lives,
that your name may be praised;
for you are our God.
Amen.

Talking points
❖ our experience of television news;
❖ the power of communication;
❖ broadcasting how much Jesus has done for us.

Activity for younger children
Make a cardboard box television. Ask an adult to cut a hole in the bottom of a large cardboard box. Paint the box. Add control panels like those on a television set. Sit behind the box and 'broadcast' your own news programmes.

This belongs to: . . . .

Make a welcome poster

You will need

poster paper   felt tip pens

What to do

Make a welcome poster to display in your entrance hall or on your bedroom door.

1.   Draw a decorative border. Write 'welcome' in the middle.
2.   Add the same message in other languages.
2.   Learn to say some of these welcome words as a greeting to visitors.

welcome
English

Fáille
Irish/Gaelic

soo dhawow
Somali

BIENVENIDOS
Spanish

willkommen
German

croeso
Welsh

benvenuti
Italian

ΚΑΡΙΒΩ
Swahili

selamat datang
Malay

bienvenue
French

vel
Romani

witajcie
Polish

hoan nghênh
Vietnamese

hos geldiniz
Turkish

**Our words make others feel welcome.
When we welcome others, we welcome Jesus.**

This belongs to: . . . .

Welcome

Today at church
Today at church we talked about our experiences of being made welcome. Then we heard how we can welcome Jesus when we welcome other people.

Gospel theme
People who welcome those whom Jesus sends welcome Jesus himself. People who welcome Jesus welcome the Father who sent him. In other words, those who are sent in Jesus' name represent Jesus in every sense of that word.

Gospel passage (Matthew 10.40–42)
Jesus said, 'Whoever welcomes you welcomes me,
and whoever welcomes me
welcomes the one who sent me.
Whoever welcomes a prophet in the name of a prophet
will receive a prophet's reward;
and whoever welcomes a righteous person
in the name of a righteous person
will receive the reward of the righteous;
and whoever gives even a cup of cold water
to one of these little ones in the name of a disciple –
truly I tell you,
none of these will lose their reward.'

Prayer
Lord Jesus Christ,
everyone who welcomes your people
welcomes you.
Help us to see you
in the people we meet,
that we may welcome you
through serving the needs of others;
today and always.
Amen.

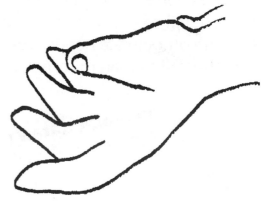

Talking points
- ❖ our experiences of being made welcome;
- ❖ how we welcome Jesus in other people;
- ❖ seeing Jesus in others.

Activity for younger children
Make a brightly coloured poster for your room. Write on it the word 'Welcome'.

This belongs to: . . . .

Play a game

You will need

    a die   paper

    pens or pencils   other players

What to do

The object of the game is to be the first to complete drawing an ambulance.

- Each number on the die represents a different part of the ambulance. As you throw that number, draw in the part. The numbers are:

      6 - ambulance body

      5 - flashing light

      4 - door

      3 - wheel

      2 - wheel

      1 - red cross

- Take turns to throw the die. You need a 6 to start.
- If you throw a number you do not need, wait for your next turn.
- The ambulance needs four wheels. You can only draw one at a time.
- The first person to complete an ambulance is the winner.

**Ambulances carry us to a place of healing.
Jesus is the great healer.**

This belongs to: . . . .

Ambulance

Today at church
Today at church we talked about our experiences of the ambulance service. Then we heard how Jesus went about making people well.

Gospel theme
Healing is a central theme in Mark's account of the ministry of Jesus. Accounts of healing begin in chapters one and two with a man with an unclean spirit, Peter's mother-in-law, a leper and a paralysed man. Now the most fundamental of healings takes place as Jairus' daughter is restored to life.

Gospel passage (Mark 5.22-24)
Then one of the leaders of the synagogue named Jairus came
and, when he saw Jesus,
fell at his feet and begged him repeatedly,
'My little daughter is at the point of death.
Come and lay your hands on her,
so that she may be made well, and live.'
So Jesus went with him.

Prayer
Lord Jesus Christ,
you brought health to the sick
and hope to the suffering.
Bless those who bring healing
in our world,
that they may live to praise your name;
now and always.
Amen.

Talking points
❖ our experiences of the ambulance service;
❖ the place of healing in the gospel;
❖ recognising Jesus the healer.

Activity for younger children
Use a cardboard box to make a model ambulance. Glue on paper doors, windows and a red cross. Add cardboard wheels.

This belongs to: . . . .

Make a treasure chest

You will need

small box

tissue paper

PVA glue

gold or silver paint

scraps of net or fine fabric

paint

What to do

1.   Paint the box with gold or silver paint.
2.   Rip the tissue paper into pieces no bigger than 10 cm square. Cut the net into pieces no bigger than 5 cm square.
3.   Pour PVA glue into a flat container. Add a very small amount of water and mix it in.
4.   Dip pieces of paper or net into the glue. Squeeze it to remove excess glue. Place it on the box and scrunch it into interesting shapes. Cover as much of the box as you wish.
5.   While the glue is still wet, add drops of paint and swirl it into the paper and fabric so the colour is mixed in a way that interests you. (If you wish you can glue on sequins or shells or beads for extra effect.)
6.   Leave the box for a few days until it is dry. You can add more gold or silver paint lightly on top of the other colours but be sparing as too much gold and silver spoils the effect.

**To find treasure we must persevere.
The Christian life requires perseverance.**

This belongs to: ....

Treasure trail

Today at church
Today at church we talked about treasure trails. Then we heard how we need to follow Jesus on the Christian life.

Gospel theme
Those who begin the journey with Jesus must commit themselves wholeheartedly to completing it. There is to be no turning back. Nor is there to be any supernatural intervention to make the going easy.

Gospel passage (Luke 9.57–58)
As they were going along the road, someone said to him,
'I will follow you wherever you go.'
And Jesus said to him,
'Foxes have holes, and birds of the air have nests;
but the Son of Man has nowhere to lay his head.'

Prayer
Lord Jesus Christ,
you call your people
to follow you wherever you lead.
Give us grace to follow you in the way,
that we may share in your kingdom;
for you are our God.
Amen.

Talking points
❖   our ideas of treasure trails;
❖   true discipleship as a treasure trail;
❖   perseverance in the Christian life.

Activity for younger children
Prepare a treasure trail in your house. Hide a 'treasure' such as sweets for everyone to share. Make a trail leading to it. The trail can be of small pieces of paper placed some distance apart so your family needs to keep trying in order to find the treasure.

This belongs to: . . . .

Play a game

Play this game with a friend. Time yourself to see how long you enjoy playing it together.

What to do

1. Ask a friend to press in a three digit number on a calculator and then to repeat the digits to make a six digit number (such as 352,352). Keep your back turned so that you cannot see the number.
2. Ask your friend to divide the number by 7 and not to worry about a remainder as there will not be one.
3. Ask your friend to divide this number by 11 and again not to worry about a remainder as there will not be one.
4. Ask your friend to divide this number by 13, and again there will be no remainder.
5. The answer will be the three digit number your friend first keyed in.
6. Try it with several different numbers to be sure it always works.

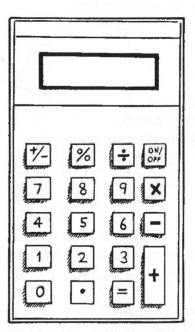

We may reject friends' ideas of games.
We welcome Jesus.

This belongs to: ....

Children's games

Today at church
Today at church we talked about all kinds of children's games. Then we heard how the people criticised the very different lifestyles of John the Baptist and Jesus.

Gospel theme
John the Baptist and Jesus presented highly contrasted images of God's messenger. John withdrew to the desert and lived as an ascetic. Jesus lived among people and drew large followings. He accepted the company of tax collectors and sinners. Both, however, were rejected by their generation.

Gospel passage (Matthew 11.16-19)
Jesus said, 'To what will I compare this generation?
It is like children sitting in the market-places
and calling to one another,
"We played the flute for you, and you did not dance;
we wailed, and you did not mourn."
For John came neither eating nor drinking,
and they say, "He has a demon";
the Son of Man came eating and drinking,
and they say, "Look, a glutton and a drunkard,
a friend of tax-collectors and sinners!"'

Prayer
Lord Jesus Christ,
you taught your followers
to love life and to do good.
Teach us to love what is good,
that we may live our lives to your glory;
now and always.
Amen.

Talking points
* our experiences of children playing games;
* how the people rejected both John and Jesus;
* the positive aspects of John's and Jesus' styles.

Activity for younger children
Keep a record of how many games you play today. Each time you start a different game, put a counter or block in a jar. At bedtime, count the blocks to see how many different games you have played.

This belongs to: . . . .

Light luggage

How light do you travel each day?

Weigh your school bag each day for a week. Stand on a set of bathroom scales, first with your bag and then without your bag. The difference between the two weights is that of your bag.

For a healthy back, your bag should not weigh more than a tenth of your own body weight. If your bag is too heavy, go through the contents to see if you really need to carry that much.

weight	too heavy or okay?	things to remove
Monday		
Tuesday		
Wednesday		
Thursday		
Friday		

We pack carefully for a journey.
Jesus told his disciples to travel light.

This belongs to: . . . .

Travelling light

Today at church
Today at church we talked about our experiences of packing for a journey. Then we heard how Jesus told his disciples to travel light.

Gospel theme
The twelve disciples are sent out in pairs on their first missionary journey. The urgency of the task is reflected in the way in which they are to travel light, unencumbered by unnecessary baggage and preparation.

Gospel passage (Mark 6.7-9)
Jesus called the twelve and began to send them out two by two, and gave them authority over the unclean spirits.
He ordered them to take nothing for their journey except a staff; no bread, no bag, no money in their belts;
but to wear sandals and not to put on two tunics.

Prayer
Lord Jesus Christ,
you taught your followers
to travel light in your service.
Help us to follow in their footsteps,
that we are not weighed down
with the baggage of life;
for you are our God.
Amen.

Talking points
❖ our experiences of packing for a journey;
❖ the disciples' need to travel light;
❖ travelling light in the service of Jesus.

Activity for younger children
Pack a case or a rucksack with the things you would want to take if you were going away for two days. Weigh your bag. Are you travelling light? Try walking around the house for ten minutes carrying the bag.

This belongs to: . . . .

Send a secret message

Make a tetra-tetraflexagon with a secret message.

What to do

1. Rule a piece of paper or thin card into 12 squares. (A sheet of A4 paper divides into 12 squares of 7 cm if you cut off the end.) Number the squares or colour each set of numbers a different colour, and write a secret message about Jesus on the question mark squares.
2. Cut along the three heavy lines and fold these two centre squares back.
3. Fold back the column on the extreme right.
4. Fold back the column on the right again.
5. The single square on the left should be folded forward and to the right (around the column on the left). All six of the '1' squares should be on the front. Fasten together the centre edges with clear sticky tape as shown.
6. Turn over and you will see all six of the '2' squares. Flex different sections over until you can see all six of the '3' squares. Then keep flexing to find the secret message.
7. Give your tetra-tetraflexagon to a friend, suggesting that they look for a secret message inside.

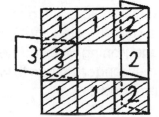
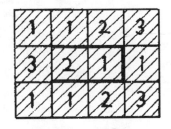
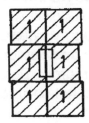

> **Jesus sent out 70 messengers.**
> **We can share in their work by telling of Jesus.**

This belongs to: ....

Messengers

Today at church
Today at church we talked about messengers. Then we heard how Jesus sent seventy people ahead of him to prepare for his own arrival in the towns and villages.

Gospel theme
Luke tells how Jesus sent the seventy followers on a missionary journey. They are to carry no purse, no bag, no sandals, and to greet no one on the road. Haste and speed are all important.

Gospel passage (Luke 10.1-2)
The Lord appointed seventy others
and sent them on ahead of him in pairs
to every town and place where he himself intended to go.
He said to them,
'The harvest is plentiful, but the labourers are few;
therefore ask the Lord of the harvest
to send out labourers into his harvest.'

Prayer
Lord Jesus Christ,
you sent your messengers
to prepare the way before you.
Send us out in your name
to share your good news with others,
that all may hear of your love and power;
for you are our God.
Amen.

Talking points
❖   our experiences of messengers;
❖   the seventy as Jesus' messengers;
❖   sharing in the work of the seventy.

Activity for younger children
Be a messenger and deliver items like the ironing and the newspaper to other members of your family. Design special messenger clothes to wear for your work. Decorate a paper hat and make paper armbands.

This belongs to: . . . .

Experiment with seeds

You will need

seeds   pots and soil

saucer   cotton wool

What to do

1. Prepare four or five different environments in which to grow seeds.
   - Plant the first set of seeds in a weedy patch of the garden.
   - Plant the second set of seeds in a pot of soil and keep it in a warm, dark airing cupboard.
   - Plant the third set of seeds in a pot of soil on a sunny window ledge.
   - Plant the fourth set of seeds on cotton wool in a saucer and keep it on a sunny window ledge.
   - Plant the fifth set of seeds in an open patch of garden.
2. Treat each environment the same way. Water it at the same time and with the same amount of water. (Use a measuring jug to be sure.)
3. Keep watch on the seeds to see how well they grow. Which seeds grow well? Which seeds do not grow at all?
4. Compare your findings with Jesus' story in Matthew 13.1-9.

 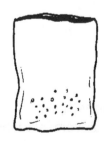 

Soil, water and light help plants to grow.
The kingdom of God grows with our help.

This belongs to: . . . .

Farmer

Today at church
Today at church we talked about farmers. Then we listened to Jesus' story about the farmer who went out to sow seed on his land.

Gospel theme
The well known parable of the sower teaches that the kingdom of God grows like seed. Those who wish to understand the kingdom of God must begin by understanding how things work in the natural world which God created.

Gospel passage (Matthew 13.3-8)
Jesus said, 'Listen! A sower went out to sow.
And as he sowed, some seeds fell on the path,
and the birds came and ate them up.
Other seeds fell on rocky ground,
where they did not have much soil,
and they sprang up quickly,
since they had no depth of soil.
But when the sun rose, they were scorched;
and since they had no root, they withered away.
Other seeds fell among thorns,
and the thorns grew up and choked them.
Other seeds fell on good soil and brought forth grain,
some a hundredfold, some sixty, some thirty.'

Prayer
Lord Jesus Christ,
you have sown the word of life in our hearts.
Give us grace to nurture the seed,
that we may be fruitful in your service;
today and every day.
Amen.

Talking points
❖ our experience of farmers;
❖ the natural processes of growth;
❖ the link between the natural world and the kingdom of God.

Activity for younger children
Plant some seeds. Put half of the seeds in a pot of soil and water them regularly. Put the other half on a saucer without soil or water. What difference does it make?

This belongs to: . . . .

Paint a picture

Think about this

There are different types of pain:

- physical - hurting the body (hitting, kicking)
- emotional - hurting the feelings ('I hate you!', 'You're horrid!')
- intellectual - hurting the mind ('You're wrong!', 'You can't add up!')

This week, take notice of times when people cause pain to you or to those around you, or when you cause pain to others. Think about ways the pain could have been avoided. What could have been said or done instead?

What to do

1. Think about how you feel when someone causes you pain. Some people do not notice one kind of pain; other people notice all three types. Do you feel more hurt by one type than another?
2. Write down words or actions that cause you pain. Paint a picture to express your feelings at these. You could paint a picture for each of the different types of pain.

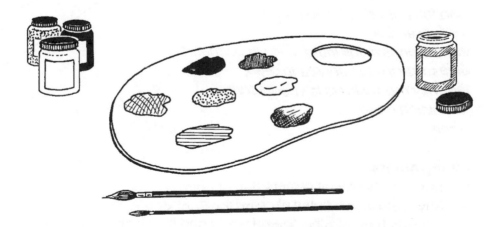

> We feel pain when people treat us unkindly.
> Jesus' disciples knew pain from following him.

This belongs to: . . . .

Pain

Today at church
Today at church we talked about our experiences of pain. Then we heard how John the Baptist was put to death.

Gospel theme
By telling about the death of John the Baptist, Mark illustrates a major point. Just as John endured pain through preaching the gospel, and just as Jesus endured pain, so the disciples can expect the same reception for their ministry.

Gospel passage (Mark 6.22-24)
When his daughter Herodias came in and danced,
she pleased Herod and his guests;
and the king said to the girl,
'Ask me for whatever you wish, and I will give it.'
And he solemnly swore to her,
'Whatever you ask me, I will give you,
even half of my kingdom.'
She went out and said to her mother,
'What should I ask for?'
She replied,
'The head of John the Baptist.'

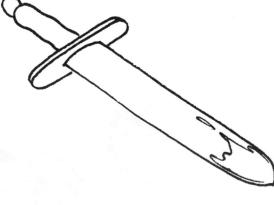

Prayer
Lord Jesus Christ,
John the Baptist suffered martyrdom
in your service.
Stand alongside all those
who suffer in your service today,
that they may witness to your glory;
now and always.
Amen.

Talking points
❖   our experiences of the infliction of pain;
❖   how pain was inflicted on John the Baptist;
❖   the death of John the Baptist.

Activity for younger children
Make a paper plate mask to show how you feel when you see someone causing pain to a friend, or how you feel when someone causes you pain. Cut out holes for eyes. Draw on the rest of the face. Attach elastic or ribbon to hold the mask on your face.

This belongs to: . . . .

Make chocolate balls to give away

You will need

250 g sweet biscuits   80 g coconut
2 tablespoons cocoa   400 g tin sweetened condensed milk
vanilla essence   extra coconut or chocolate splinters

What to do

1. Place the biscuits in 2 plastic bags. Crush them into small pieces with a rolling pin or your hands.
2. Place the biscuits in a bowl with the coconut and cocoa and mix well.
3. Add a few drops of vanilla essence and stir in the condensed milk.
4. Form the mixture into small balls. (You should make about 40 or 50 balls.) Roll the balls in coconut or chocolate splinters. Place the balls on a plate or tray and refrigerate until set.
5. Arrange the chocolate balls on a paper plate or dish and give them to a neighbour as a sign of respect and love.

We can be good neighbours.
God cares about our neighbours.

This belongs to: . . . .

Neighbours

Today at church
Today at church we talked about all the different people living in our neighbourhood. Then we heard how the good Samaritan was a proper neighbour to the man who was robbed and beaten up on the Jericho road.

Gospel theme
In the parable of the Good Samaritan the traveller is left for dead. The priest and Levite pass by because contact with a corpse would have made them ritually unclean. The Samaritan who helps is a foreigner and an outcast. Jesus tells us to follow that Samaritan's example.

Gospel passage (Luke 10.30, 33-34)
Jesus replied,
'A man was going down from Jerusalem to Jericho,
and fell into the hands of robbers,
who stripped him, beat him, and went away,
leaving him half dead.
But a Samaritan while travelling came near him;
and when he saw him, he was moved with pity.
He went to him and bandaged his wounds,
having poured oil and wine on them.
Then he put him on his own animal,
brought him to an inn, and took care of him.'

Prayer
Lord Jesus Christ,
you teach your disciples
to follow the example of the good Samaritan.
Help us to respond to the needs of others,
that we may show your love to the world;
for you are our God.
Amen.

Talking points
* ❖ the people living in our neighbourhood;
* ❖ God cares for our neighbours;
* ❖ respect and love for our neighbours.

Activity for younger children
Watch your neighbours and find out about things they do, such as walk the dog, wash the car, water the garden. Make a book with a different page for each neighbour, for example, 'Mrs Owens works in her garden.'

This belongs to: . . . .

Make a summer scene collage

You will need

long sheet of backing paper   coloured paper or fabric
scissors   glue

What to do

1. Find a long sheet of strong paper to use as a backing for a collage.
2. Cut or tear green paper or fabric to form a grassy background of hills (countryside scene) or park.
3. Add brown paper tree trunks and green leaves. Add brightly coloured flower beds. Flowers can be made from paper stalks and fabric petals.
4. Add birds and animals that are found in parks and the country in summer.
5. Display the collage at home to remind yourself of signs of God's activity and presence in the world around you.

**The world is full of signs of God's work.
We remember God as we look around us.**

This belongs to: . . . .

Summer walk

Today at church
Today at church we talked about taking a summer walk in the park or countryside and looking for all the signs of God's activity around us. Then we heard how Jesus used everyday experiences like this in his teaching about the kingdom of God.

Gospel theme
Jesus had a very keen eye for all that was going on around him, as he observed the natural processes in nature. His audience identified with what he was describing because they lived in the same world themselves. But then comes the twist in the tale, as Jesus applies the knowledge they already have to a new situation and opens their eyes to new insight.

Gospel passage (Matthew 13.24-26)
Jesus put before the crowd another parable:
'The kingdom of heaven may be compared
to someone who sowed good seed in his field;
but while everybody was asleep,
an enemy came and sowed weeds among the wheat, and then went away.
So when the plants came up and bore grain
then the weeds appeared as well.'

Prayer
Lord God,
the signs of your activity are all around us.
Open our eyes to the secrets of your kingdom,
that we may know your ways
and experience your love;
now and always.
Amen.

Talking points
❖ walking in countryside or park and being alert to all around us;
❖ looking for signs of God's activity and presence;
❖ Jesus applied everyday experiences to the kingdom of God.

Activity for younger children
Make a shoe box model of a park. Glue green paper to the inside of a box (or paint it green). Make paper trees and flower beds to glue in. Add small animals and birds.

This belongs to: . . . .

Make a 'fan wall'

You will need

picture of Jesus   streamers
balloons   paper
pens   Bible

What to do

1. Fans decorate their rooms in honour of football players or pop stars. You could decorate part of your room to honour Jesus.
2. Choose a suitable wall in your room. Find or paint a picture of Jesus to put in the centre. (Make sure you put it up with an adhesive that does not mark the paint or wallpaper.)
3. Surround the picture with coloured streamers. Add balloons and special messages such as 'I'm in Jesus' fan club' or 'Jesus forever'.
4. If you have a table or desk near that wall, put a Bible on it and keep a vase of fresh flowers nearby.

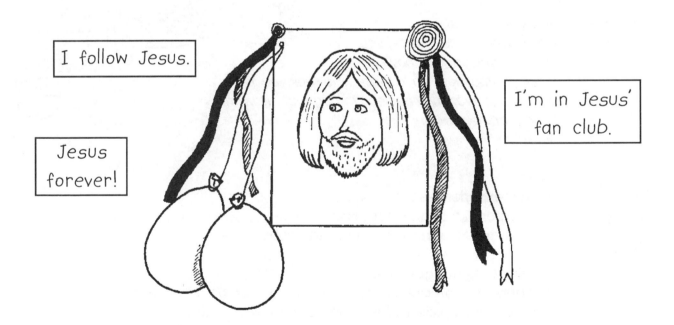

I follow Jesus.

Jesus forever!

I'm in Jesus' fan club.

**People were eager to follow Jesus.
We can be part of Jesus' fan club today.**

This belongs to: . . . .

Fan club

Today at church

Today at church we talked about our experiences of fan clubs. Then we heard how people showed their enthusiasm for Jesus when he visited their shore.

Gospel theme

Throughout his gospel, Mark draws a clear contrast between the reception given to Jesus by the Jewish leaders and the reception given to him by the common people. We are shown how the common people flocked around Jesus, to the point that Jesus and his disciples had no leisure even to eat.

Gospel passage (Mark 6.54-56)

When they got out of the boat,
people at once recognised Jesus,
and rushed about that whole region
and began to bring the sick on mats to wherever they heard he was.
And wherever he went, into villages or cities or farms,
they laid the sick in the market-places,
and begged him that they might touch even the fringe of his cloak;
and all who touched it were healed.

Prayer

Lord Jesus Christ,
the crowds came to meet you
and recognised your power.
Make yourself known to those who seek you today,
that your power may be seen throughout the world;
for you are our God.
Amen.

Talking points

- ❖ our experiences of fan clubs;
- ❖ the popular support for Jesus;
- ❖ committing ourselves to Jesus' fan club.

Activity for younger children

Members of a fan club display pictures. You can be a member of Jesus' fan club. Draw or paint a picture of Jesus to display in your room.

This belongs to: . . . .

Investigate jobs

Think

- Who does the difficult jobs at your house?
- Who gets the special tasks to do?
- Are they shared equally between younger and older family members?
- Are they shared equally between males and females?

What to do

1. This week make a list of all the tasks that are done in your house. Next to each task write who does it.
2. At the end of the week discuss your list with other family members.
    - Is it fair?
    - Should you help anyone who has too many tasks?
    - Is everyone given an equal opportunity to help?
    - Does everyone do some difficult tasks and some fun tasks?
    - Are there any tasks that are only done by women or girls?
    - Are there any tasks that are only done by men or boys?
    - Should you swap some tasks around?
3. Work together to make up a list of jobs that is more fair.

Jobs	Who does them?
set the table	
cook	
empty bin	
feed guinea pig	
clean	
mow lawn	
make the bed	

**Jesus gave equal opportunities to men and women.
We can encourage fairness.**

This belongs to: ....

Equal opportunities

Today at church
Today at church we talked about the importance of equal opportunities for all people and the need to respect different choices people make. Then we heard about the different choices made by Mary and Martha when Jesus visited their house.

Gospel theme
Women are given a particularly prominent role in Luke's gospel, as Luke demonstrates how Jesus challenged the assumptions of his age which regarded women as inferior to men. In the present story Mary 'sat at the Lord's feet', like a male pupil being instructed by the rabbi.

Gospel passage (Luke 10.38-40)
Now as Jesus and his disciples went on their way,
he entered a certain village,
where a woman named Martha welcomed him into her home.
She had a sister named Mary,
who sat at the Lord's feet and listened to what he was saying.
But Martha was distracted by her many tasks;
so she came to Jesus and asked,
'Lord, do you not care
that my sister has left me to do all the work by myself?
Tell her then to help me.'

Prayer
Lord Jesus Christ,
you welcomed the invitation
into the home of Mary and Martha.
Come into our homes
and shape our lives,
that we may listen to your words
and serve you as you desire;
now and always.
Amen.

Talking points
❖   our experiences of equal opportunities;
❖   Jesus' attitude towards women;
❖   equal opportunities and respect in the church.

Activity for younger children
Is there anything that you really want to do and people say 'Only girls do that' or 'Only boys do that'? This is your opportunity to try it out. As part of thinking about equal opportunities, plan a time when you can do as you wish.

This belongs to: . . . .

Make a lucky dip

You will need

large box

sawdust, polystyrene or paper

presents or sweets

What to do

1. Fill a large box with sawdust or polystyrene packing or strips of paper.
2. Add some 'treasure' - small wrapped presents or sweets. Mix everything together well.
3. Invite family and friends to hunt in the box for the hidden treasure.

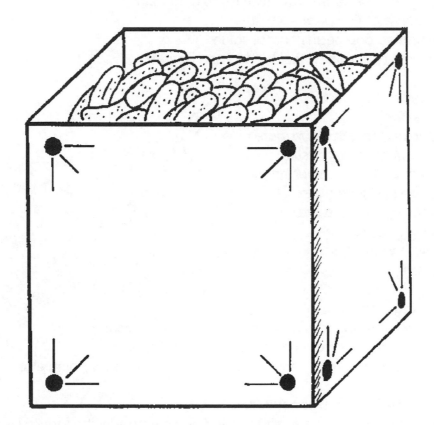

**The kingdom of heaven is like buried treasure.
It is worth more than everything else.**

This belongs to: . . . .

Hidden treasure

Today at church
Today at church we talked about hidden treasure. Then we heard Jesus' story about the man who bought a field because of the hidden treasure in it.

Gospel theme
The parable of the hidden treasure, which is told only in Matthew's gospel, points to the experience of the disciples. They, too, have found treasure in Jesus and left all that they had to follow him.

Gospel passage (Matthew 13.44–46)
Jesus said, 'The kingdom of heaven is like treasure hidden in a field,
which someone found and hid;
then in his joy he goes and sells all that he has
and buys that field.
Again, the kingdom of heaven is like a merchant
in search of fine pearls;
on finding one pearl of great value,
he went and sold all that he had and bought it.'

Prayer
Lord God,
your kingdom is worth more
than all human treasure.
Teach us to value your kingdom
above everything else,
that we give ourselves
to your service;
now and always.
Amen.

Talking points
❖ our experiences and images of hidden treasure;
❖ the kingdom of heaven as hidden treasure;
❖ the kingdom of heaven as worth more than everything else.

Activity for younger children
Play 'Hunt the treasure' with a friend or a member of the family. Hide a small object for someone else to find. You can give clues if you wish.

This belongs to: . . . .

Cook chapattis

You will need

½ cup wholemeal flour   ½ cup white flour
water

What to do

This mixture makes two chapattis. For four chapattis, double the flour.

1. Mix the flour together. Add enough water to make a soft dough that does not stick to your hands. Leave it for 5 minutes.
2. Form the mixture into two round balls. Place them on a floured board or bench and flatten them with a rolling pin.
3. Heat a non-stick frying pan. Add one chapatti and leave it to cook. Turn it over once to cook both sides. Press it down to flatten it if needed. Cook the second chapatti in the same way.
4. Serve the chapattis with curry or mince.

**Bread is eaten all across the world.
Jesus is concerned that people are fed.**

This belongs to: . . . .

World breads

Today at church
Today at church we talked about the many different forms of bread in the local shops and across the world. Then we heard about Jesus' concern that the people who came to hear him should be fed.

Gospel theme
The story of the feeding of the five thousand is told in all four gospels. John's account emphasises Jesus' concern that the people who come to hear him should be fed.

Gospel passage (John 6.10–11)
Jesus said, 'Make the people sit down.'
Now there was a great deal of grass in the place;
so they sat down, about five thousand in all.
Then Jesus took the loaves,
and when he had given thanks,
he distributed them to those who were seated;
so also the fish, as much as they wanted.

Prayer
Lord Jesus Christ,
you fed the five thousand people
with five loaves and two fish.
Have pity on those who go hungry,
that the food of the world
may be shared more fairly;
for you are the bread of life.
Amen.

Talking points
❖ our experiences of different forms of bread;
❖ bread as a basic human food across the world;
❖ Jesus' concern with people being fed.

Activity for younger children
Draw pictures of five small rolls and two fish. Cut these out and glue them to a paper plate or onto a picture of a lunchbox. Remember the boy who shared his lunch with Jesus and five thousand people.

This belongs to: . . . .

The Lord's Prayer

Think

The church is the family of God.
You are part of the worldwide Christian family.
All Christians pray the Lord's prayer.

What to do

Make a decorated version of the Lord's prayer to display in your room.

1.   Copy the words of the Lord's prayer onto a large sheet of paper.
2.   Add a colourful border.
3.   Display it in your room. When you read it, remember that you are part of the worldwide Christian family, praying the family prayer of God's people.

Our Father in heaven,
hallowed be your name,
your kingdom come,
your will be done,
on earth as in heaven.
Give us today our daily bread.
Forgive us our sins
as we forgive those who sin against us.
Lead us not into temptation
but deliver us from evil.

For the kingdom, the power,
  and the glory are yours
now and for ever. Amen.

**We are part of the family with whom we live.
We are part of the world-wide Christian family.**

This belongs to: . . . .

Family

Today at church
Today at church we talked about the wider families to which we belong and how the church is a worldwide family. Then we heard how Jesus taught his disciples the family prayer of the church.

Gospel theme
Both Matthew and Luke record Jesus as teaching his disciples what has become known as the Lord's prayer. The Lord's prayer has become the family prayer of the Christian community, uniting Christians of many races across the world and across the generations.

Gospel passage (Luke 11.1-4)
Jesus was praying in a certain place,
and after he had finished, one of his disciples said to him,
'Lord, teach us to pray,
as John taught his disciples.'
He said to them, 'When you pray, say:
Father, hallowed be your name.
Your kingdom come.
Give us each day our daily bread.
And forgive us our sins,
for we ourselves forgive everyone indebted to us.
And do not bring us to the time of trial.'

Prayer
Lord Jesus Christ,
you taught your disciples to pray
as the family of God.
Help us to feel part of your worldwide family,
that we share with all your people
in offering praise to your name;
today and every day.
Amen.

Talking points
❖ our ideas about family identity and loyalty;
❖ the worldwide Christian family;
❖ our place in the worldwide Christian family.

Activity for younger children
Decorate a photo frame for a family photograph. Ask an older person to cut out a cardboard frame to go around a photograph. Make the frame about 4 cm wide. Decorate it with pasta shapes or twists of paper then paint over these.

This belongs to: . . . .

Plan a picnic

What to do

1. Ask a parent or guardian if you can plan a picnic lunch for next week. Offer to be responsible for planning the meal, making a shopping list and preparing everything.

2. First, plan the menu. What would you like to eat? Think of food that can be easily prepared and will not spoil if it is squashed. What will you take to drink? Write out a menu.

3. Check the kitchen cupboards. What food do you already have? Mark it with a special sticker so that no one eats it between now and your picnic. Write out a shopping list of the food you do not have and ask for it to be bought.

4. What else will you need? Make a list of plates, cups, cutlery, paper napkins, wet cloths, drinking flasks and anything else you may need.

5. Check the cupboards again. Take out what you can and put it in a basket or bag. Write a list of last-minute things to collect. Add others to a shopping list.

6. On the morning of the picnic, prepare the food and pack the picnic basket. Check your menu and packing list to be sure you have remembered to pack everything. Have a great time!

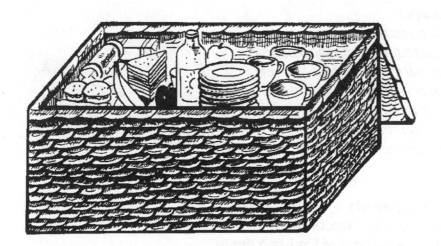

We eat with others at a picnic.
We share with others in the eucharist.

This belongs to: . . . .

Picnic

Today at church
Today at church we talked about times when we have been on picnics. Then we heard how Jesus shared food with five thousand people who ate with him in the open countryside.

Gospel theme
All four gospels relate an account of Jesus feeding the five thousand. On the one hand, this narrative looks back to the way in which Moses fed the Israelites on manna in the wilderness. On the other hand, this narrative looks forward to the way in which Jesus feeds his followers at the last supper and in the eucharist.

Gospel passage (Matthew 14.19-21)
Jesus ordered the crowds to sit down on the grass.
Taking the five loaves and the two fish,
he looked up to heaven,
and blessed and broke the loaves,
and gave them to the disciples,
and the disciples gave them to the crowds.
And all ate and were filled;
and they took up what was left over of the broken pieces,
twelve baskets full.
And those who ate were about five thousand men,
besides women and children.

Prayer
Lord Jesus Christ,
you fed five thousand people
with five loaves and two fish.
Inspire your people today,
to share the riches of your food
throughout the world;
for you are the Bread of Life.
Amen.

Talking points
❖ our experiences of picnics;
❖ the feeding of the five thousand;
❖ sharing in the eucharist.

Activity for younger children
Enjoy a picnic snack with friends or toys. Gather together food, drink, paper plates, cups and paper napkins. Find a comfortable place outside to enjoy the picnic.

This belongs to: . . . .

Investigate

Think

What happens when you keep food past its sell-by date? Does it matter? Is it different with different foods?

What to do

1. Collect small amounts of milk, bread, cheese, and any other food. Put each food in a different plastic bag or container. On the front put a label with its sell-by date. Store it in the refrigerator or cupboard, wherever that food is normally kept.
2. Check on the food again on its sell-by date. Examine it and smell it. Has there been any change?
3. Check the food each day after that. How does it change?

> **Some food does not last long.**
> **Jesus is the bread of life who lasts eternally.**

This belongs to: . . . .

Sell-by date

Today at church
Today at church we talked about the sell-by and eat-by dates on so many foods we buy in the shops. Then we heard how Jesus taught about the food that does not perish but leads to eternal life.

Gospel theme
In John's gospel the feeding of the five thousand opens the way for Jesus to teach about himself as the bread of life. In this teaching Jesus contrasts the need for physical food with the need for spiritual food.

Gospel passage (John 6.27, 33–35)
Jesus said, 'Do not work for the food that perishes,
but for the food that endures for eternal life,
which the Son of Man will give you.
For the bread of God
is that which comes down
from heaven and gives life to the world.'
They said to him,
'Sir, give us this bread always.'
Jesus said to them,
'I am the bread of life.
Whoever comes to me will never be hungry,
and whoever believes in me will never be thirsty.'

Prayer
Lord Jesus Christ,
you taught your people
to work for the things that last.
Give us grace to follow your teaching,
that we may share with you
the things that really matter;
for you are the Bread of Life.
Amen.

Talking points
❖ our experiences of sell-by dates;
❖ distinguish between what perishes and what lasts;
❖ the food that endures to eternal life.

Activity for younger children
Look through the refrigerator to find the sell-by dates on the food. Choose one food, such as milk. Pour a little of it into a container and keep it past the sell-by date. Check it every day to see how it changes.

This belongs to: . . . .

Make a money box

You will need

card   scissors
pens or pencils   sticky-tape or glue

What to do

1. Cut out the large triangle below. Fold back the shaded tab.
2. Trace around the triangle in the centre of a sheet of card. This will be the base of the money box.
3. Unfold the tab. Place this triangle plus tab so that one of the straight edges touches an edge of the base triangle. Draw around it. Repeat this with all three edges of the base triangle.
4. Decorate the shape and cut it out. Cut a rectangular hole in the top of one triangle, large enough to take coins.
5. Fold along each of the dotted lines in the illustration below to make a pyramid. Fold back the tabs. Glue the tabs to join the pyramid.
6. Use this as a money box for spare change. When the box is full, give the money to a charity for people in need.

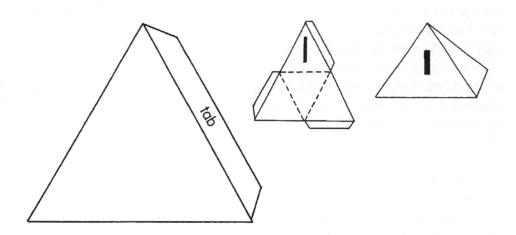

We use money every day.
Jesus said we should treat it wisely.

This belongs to: . . . .

Money

Today at church
Today at church we talked about money and why money is so important to us. Then we listened to Jesus' story about the rich man who built a bigger barn.

Gospel theme
The parable of the rich fool illustrates how wealth and possessions can become a distraction from the things that really matter in life. The rich fool made the mistake of thinking that he owned a great deal and that, as a consequence, he was most secure. The truth of the matter was that he did not even own his own life.

Gospel passage (Luke 12.16-20)
Then Jesus told them a parable:
The land of a rich man produced abundantly.
And he thought to himself,
"What should I do, for I have no place to store my crops?"
Then he said, "I will do this:
I will pull down my barns and build larger ones,
and there I will store all my grain and my goods.
And I will say to my soul,
Soul, you have ample goods laid up for many years;
relax, eat, drink, be merry."'
But God said to him,
'You fool!
This very night your life is being demanded of you.'

Prayer
Lord Jesus Christ,
you teach your people
that wealth does not last forever.
Give us a proper attitude
towards our wealth and possessions,
that we may value the things which last;
for you are our God.
Amen.

Talking points
❖ our experiences of money;
❖ Jesus' attitude towards money;
❖ a proper attitude towards money.

Activity for younger children
Borrow some coins. Put them on a table or bench and place a piece of paper over the top of them. Rub over the top of them with a crayon or pencil and watch how the coin design is transferred to the paper. Experiment with how firmly or lightly you need to press.

This belongs to: . . . .

Fold a paper boat

You will need
    A4 paper

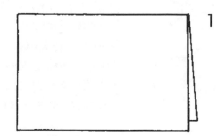

What to do

1.   Fold a sheet of paper in half.

2.   With the fold upwards, fold the two top corners down so that they meet along the centre.

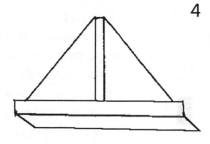

3.   Fold the top flap forward to hold the sails in place.

4.   Fold the bottom flap back to match.

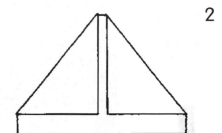

5.   Slightly open out the boat along the bottom, so that it stands.

6.   Try sailing your boat in a plastic bowl. Blow on the boat and the water to make a gale. See how the boat reacts. Would you like to be in it?

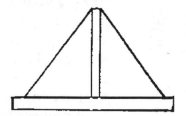

> **Jesus travelled on the way to the cross.**
> **The crowd welcomed him by throwing cloaks.**

This belongs to: . . . .

Gales

Today at church
Today at church we talked about strong winds and gales. Then we heard how Jesus stilled the strong wind which threatened the disciples' boat.

Gospel theme
After feeding the five thousand Jesus sends the disciples back into the boat and he withdraws up the mountain to pray. The winds rise quickly, the sea is stirred up and the disciples are afraid. Jesus comes to them through the gale and the winds drop. Here is good evidence that Jesus does not desert his disciples in their hour of need when buffeted by the gales of life.

Gospel passage (Matthew 14.29-32)
So Peter got out of the boat,
started walking on the water, and came towards Jesus.
But when he noticed the strong wind,
he became frightened, and beginning to sink,
he cried out, 'Lord, save me!'
Jesus immediately reached out his hand and caught him,
saying to him, 'You of little faith, why did you doubt?'
When they got into the boat, the wind ceased.

Prayer
Lord Jesus Christ,
you came to Peter
when he was in distress.
Come to us when we are battered by the storms of life,
that we may grasp your steady hand;
for you are our God.
Amen.

Talking points
❖   our experiences of gales;
❖   the gale as an image for times of stress;
❖   confidence that Jesus will still the gales.

Activity for younger children
Float a plastic boat in a baby's bath or a washing up bowl. Blow through a straw to make a gale. See the effects on the boat.

This belongs to: . . . .

Make a plaster plaque

You will need

polystyrene tray

bent wire

paints

Plaster of Paris

scratching tool

paintbrush

What to do

1. Mix up a small amount of Plaster of Paris according to the directions on the packet. Pour it into a small polystyrene tray (vegetable tray).
2. Bend some wire (such as a paperclip) to use as a hanger for the plaque. Push it over the top of the tray and into the plaster. (You can bend the wire to keep it in place and straighten it when it is set.)
3. Leave the plaque until the plaster is completely set, then remove it from the tray.
4. Use a sharp tool (such as a metal skewer or the point of a fork for the edges, and a spoon for the inside) to scratch out the shape of a communion plate and cup. (Plan your design before you begin work.) You could also scratch out words such as 'Jesus is the bread of life.'
5. Paint the scratched-out design, leaving the background as white plaster. You will need a lot of paint as it soaks in. (Bright paints and gold and silver look very effective.)
6. Display the plaque at home.

Jesus fed bread to five thousand people.
At communion we feed on Jesus, the bread of life.

This belongs to: . . . .

Communion bread

Today at church
Today at church we talked about the bread used in the communion. Then we listened to John's gospel where Jesus calls himself the Bread of Life.

Gospel theme
After feeding the five thousand, Jesus teaches that he is the bread of life. Now this teaching about the bread of life is linked directly to the church's experience of the eucharist or communion.

Gospel passage (John 6.35, 48–51)
Jesus said, 'I am the bread of life.
Your ancestors ate the manna in the wilderness, and they died.
This is the bread that comes down from heaven,
so that one may eat of it and not die.
I am the living bread that came down from heaven.
Whoever eats of this bread will live for ever;
and the bread that I will give for the life of the world
is my flesh.'

Prayer
Lord Jesus Christ,
you feed your people
in the holy communion.
Come and stand among us
when the bread is broken
and when the wine is poured,
that we may know your presence;
for you are the Bread of Life.
Amen.

Talking points
❖ our experiences of the communion bread;
❖ the links between feeding the five thousand and the communion bread;
❖ feeding on Jesus, the bread of life.

Activity for younger children
Decorate a paper plate with foil to look like the communion plate.

This belongs to: . . . .

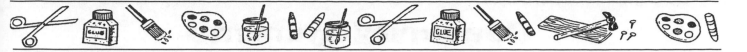

Make a model security camera

You will need

cardboard boxes and cylinders   scissors
tape or glue   paint
string

What to do

1. Think of the security cameras you have seen in shops and offices. Select a rectangular box as a base.
2. Attach a cylinder (such as a toilet roll) for the lens of the camera. Add clear plastic or cellophane or cling film to the end of the cylinder as the glass.
3. Make a frame to go on the wall and a support to join these together. Add string as the electricity cable.
4. Paint the security camera.
5. Mount the camera on the wall of your bedroom. Add a warning notice to the door.

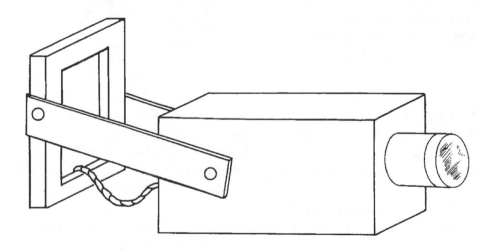

Security systems watch for danger.
Jesus said we should watch and be ready for his return.

This belongs to: . . . .

Security system

Today at church
Today at church we talked about the security systems people have in their cars, their houses and their places of work. Then we listened to Jesus' teaching about the need to be prepared for his coming.

Gospel theme
All three synoptic gospels portray Jesus issuing clear warnings to his followers to be alert and prepared. It is like a house owner being alert against the thief.

Gospel passage (Luke 12.39-40)
Jesus said, 'But know this:
if the owner of the house
had known at what hour the thief was coming,
he would not have let his house be broken into.
You also must be ready,
for the Son of Man is coming at an unexpected hour.'

Prayer
Lord Jesus Christ,
you call your people
to be ready for your coming.
Prepare our hearts,
that we may be ready for you;
for you are our God.
Amen.

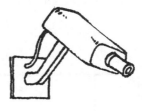

Talking points
❖   our experiences of security systems;
❖   the gospel message to be watchful;
❖   being prepared and ready for the Son of Man.

Activity for younger children
Walk through a shopping centre looking for security cameras. Imagine you are the camera and work out what you could see from that position.

This belongs to: . . . .

Make a barrier

You will need

cardboard box   felt tip pens

What to do

1. Find a large cardboard box, big enough to act as a barrier in a doorway.

2. On one side of the box write down a few words that cause barriers between people - words about their hair, skin, work or character, or about your feelings.

3. On the opposite side of the box write words that can break down barriers, words such as 'Come in', 'Welcome', 'I like your . . .' and 'You can join us'. Think of as many words or phrases as you can.

4. When you feel angry with people, put the box in the doorway of your room as a barrier, with the angry words facing out. Stand on the other side of the box and read the friendly words to yourself. Remember that you can say these at any time and remove the barrier.

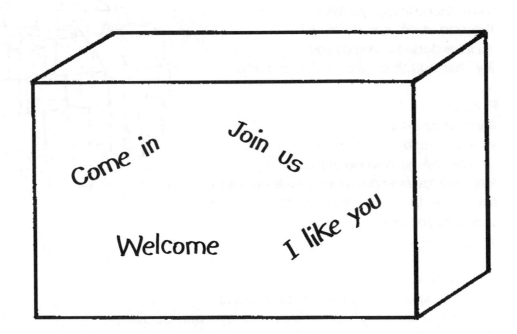

Jesus removed barriers between Jews and Gentiles. We can remove barriers that keep us apart.

This belongs to: . . . .

Removing barriers

Today at church
Today at church we talked about the effect of removing barriers. Then we heard how Jesus removed the barriers between the Gentiles and the Jews.

Gospel theme
Jesus lived in a society in which the Jewish sense of being God's chosen people built a strong barrier between the Jewish people and the rest of the world, the Gentile nations. Jesus' encounter with the Canaanite woman and with her faith shows that the barrier can be dissolved and the good news of the kingdom extended to Gentiles as well as to Jews.

Gospel passage (Matthew 15.22, 26-28)
A Canaanite woman from that region came out
and started shouting,
'Have mercy on me, Lord, Son of David;
my daughter is tormented by a demon.'
Jesus answered, 'It is not fair to take the children's food
and throw it to the dogs.'
She said, 'Yes, Lord, yet even the dogs eat the crumbs
that fall from their master's table.'
Then Jesus answered her,
'Woman, great is your faith!
Let it be done for you as you wish.'
And her daughter was healed instantly.

Prayer
Lord Jesus Christ,
you took away the barriers
between Jews and Gentiles.
Remove the barriers which divide our world,
that all people may live to praise your name;
now and for ever.
Amen.

Talking points
❖ our experiences of removing barriers;
❖ Jesus removing barriers between Jews and Gentiles;
❖ removing barriers which still keep people apart.

Activity for younger children
Build a barrier of cardboard boxes or cushions to block a doorway. Work with a friend or someone in the family to remove the barrier. Each start at a different side of the barrier and meet in the middle.

This belongs to: . . . .

Make a communion set

You will need

paper plate	foil
scissors	glue and tape
scrap paper	card

What to do

1. Make a model of a communion plate. Start with a paper plate and cover it with foil. Crease the foil around the edges to make a raised design.

2. Use scrap paper to practise making a communion cup. Tape a piece of paper into a cylinder. Towards the bottom crease the paper to make the stem of the cup. Keep the top and bottom cylindrical. Practise creasing at different places to achieve the effect you want.

3. Cover some thin card with foil. Use this to make a model of the communion cup.

4. Display these in your room with a sign such as 'Jesus gives life.' (If you wish, these word could be written on the foil before the cup is made.)

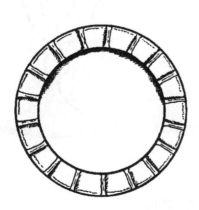

**We celebrate communion at church.
We remember Jesus came to give us life.**

This belongs to: . . . .

Communion cup

Today at church
Today at church we talked about the various communion cups used in church. Then we listened to Jesus' teaching in John's gospel about sharing the communion cup and drinking the blood of Christ.

Gospel theme
In John's gospel Jesus proclaims, 'Unless you eat the flesh of the Son of Man and drink his blood, you have no life in you.'

Gospel passage (John 6.53–56)
So Jesus said to them,
'Very truly, I tell you,
unless you eat the flesh of the Son of Man and drink his blood,
you have no life in you.
Those who eat my flesh and drink my blood have eternal life,
and I will raise them up on the last day;
for my flesh is true food and my blood is true drink.
Those who eat my flesh and drink my blood abide in me,
and I in them.'

Prayer
Lord Jesus Christ,
you teach your people
to share your bread
and to drink your cup.
Come and stand among us
when the bread is broken
and when the wine is poured,
that we may know your presence;
for you are the Bread of Life.
Amen.

Talking points
❖ our experiences of the communion cup;
❖ the communion cup as the blood of Christ;
❖ being nurtured by the blood of Christ.

Activity for younger children
Make a model of a communion cup. Cover a plastic cup or a paper cup with foil.

This belongs to: . . . .

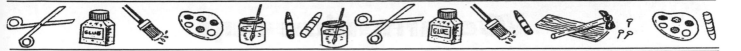

Record the weather forecast

Think

How accurate is the weather forecast?

Keep a record for a week, of the forecasts and the actual weather.

What to do

1. Make up a chart like the one below, with space for each day of the week. Draw in a column for the weather forecast and one for what the weather actually was like.

2. Each evening listen to the forecast for the next day's weather. Record it on the chart. Include details of expected temperature, rain and sun. At the end of the next day record what the weather was actually like.

3. At the end of the week, compare the forecast with the actual weather. How accurate was the forecast?

day	the weather forecast	the actual weather
Monday		
Tuesday		
Wednesday		

> **We are alert to changes in the weather.**
> **Jesus said we should be alert to the signs of the times.**

This belongs to: . . . .

Weather forecast

Today at church
Today at church we talked about the weather forecasts we see on television, hear on the radio or read in the papers. Then we listened to Jesus teaching his followers about the importance of reading the signs of the times.

Gospel theme
There is a long tradition in the Old Testament of the prophets reading the mind of God behind the signs of the time. In Luke's gospel Jesus understands his own ministry and impending suffering as signalling the moment of crisis and judgement for the Jewish people. The signs are there, if only the people would read them.

Gospel passage (Luke 12.54-56)
Jesus also said to the crowds,
'When you see a cloud rising in the west, you immediately say,
"It is going to rain";
and so it happens.
And when you see the south wind blowing, you say,
"There will be scorching heat";
and it happens.
You hypocrites!
You know how to interpret the appearance of earth and sky,
but why do you not know how to interpret the present time?'

Prayer
Lord Jesus Christ,
you teach your people
to read the signs of the times.
Open our eyes to the signs of your presence,
that we may serve you as you desire;
now and always.
Amen.

Talking points
❖ our experiences of weather forecasts;
❖ Jesus' concern with the signs of the times;
❖ being alert to the mind of God in the signs of the times.

Activity for younger children
With an adult, watch the weather forecast on television or listen to it on the radio. Write or draw the prediction for the next day's weather. Check the next day to see if it is correct.

This belongs to: . . . .

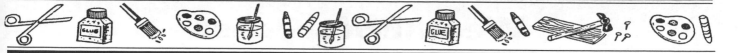

Make a rock church

You will need

rocks and pebbles   strong glue

What to do

1. Collect lots of small rocks and pebbles.
2. Use these rocks to build a model of a church.
3. Remember Jesus' saying to Peter about building his church 'on this rock'. The name Peter means 'rock'.

**Peter recognised Jesus as the Messiah.
We can worship Jesus too.**

This belongs to: . . . .

Rock

Today at church
Today at church we talked about rocks and about how rocks can be strong and stable. Then we heard how Jesus renamed Simon to be called Peter and how the name 'Peter' means 'rock'.

Gospel theme
In the gospels of Matthew, Mark and Luke, Peter's public recognition of Jesus as the Messiah at Caesarea Philippi marks a significant turning point. Jesus rewards Peter's confession of faith with the acknowledgement that this is the rock on which the church will be built.

Gospel passage (Matthew 16.15–18)
Jesus said to them, 'But who do you say that I am?'
Simon Peter answered,
'You are the Messiah, the Son of the living God.'
And Jesus answered him,
'Blessed are you, Simon son of Jonah!
For flesh and blood has not revealed this to you,
but my Father in heaven.
And I tell you, you are Peter,
and on this rock I will build my church.'

Prayer
Lord Jesus Christ,
you build your church on Peter the rock.
Give us faith like his
that we may name you
as the Christ and Saviour;
now and always.
Amen.

Talking points
❖   our experiences and images of rocks;
❖   Peter as the rock on which Jesus builds;
❖   acknowledging Jesus as Messiah, as Peter did.

Activity for younger children
Make a pet rock. Choose a rock with an interesting shape and colour. Glue on paper eyes and a mouth.

This belongs to: . . . .

Make paper poppies

You will need

light wire   scissors
cotton wool   sticky tape
green, black and red paper   glue

What to do

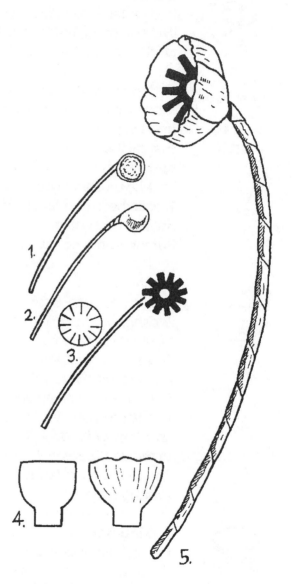

1. Cut a length of wire about 30 cm long. (If you do not have any wire, use a plastic straw and adapt some of the instructions.) Bend the top of the wire to make a small loop and fill this with cotton wool as the centre of the poppy.

2. Cut out a circle of green paper to cover the cotton wool. Hold it in place by wrapping tape around the bottom.

3. Cut two or three circles from black paper. Fringe the outer edges and slide these along the wire, from the bottom end, to the green centre.

4. Cut out five petal shapes from red paper. (Crêpe paper is best. If you have this, gently stretch the top with your fingers so that the petals frill.) Glue or tape the petals behind the black circles.

5. Cut longs strips of green paper and use these to cover the stem by winding them diagonally around the wire. Follow the instructions to make more poppies.

**Flowers are a celebration of new life.
We share in the new life of the eucharist.**

This belongs to: . . . .

Festival of flowers

Today at church

Today at church we talked about festivals of flowers and fine flower displays. Festivals of flowers can be a real celebration of life. Then we heard how Jesus promised the eucharist as a real celebration of life.

Gospel theme

In chapter 6 John has developed a clear progression of thought from feeding the five thousand, to Jesus as the bread of life, to Jesus giving his flesh for the life of the world, and to the bread and wine of the eucharist.

Gospel passage (John 6.56–58)

Jesus said, 'Those who eat my flesh and drink my blood abide in me,
and I in them.
Just as the living Father sent me,
and I live because of the Father,
so whoever eats me will live because of me.
This is the bread that came down from heaven,
not like that which your ancestors ate, and they died.
But the one who eats this bread will live for ever.'

Prayer

Thank you Lord Jesus,
for sharing bread with the five thousand
when they were hungry.
Thank you Lord Jesus,
for sharing bread with your disciples
before you suffered death.
Thank you Lord Jesus,
for sharing bread with your people
in the communion service.
Thank you Lord Jesus.
Amen.

Talking points

❖ our experiences of flower festivals;
❖ flower festivals as a celebration of new life;
❖ the new life of the eucharist.

Activity for younger children

Make paper flowers. For each flower cut out a paper circle (tissue paper is best) in two different colours. Place one circle on top of the other and fold them into quarters. Twist the narrow section to hold the two colours together and open out the top for the petals. You could make several to decorate a card.

This belongs to: . . . .

Make a helping hands mobile

You will need

card   scissors

pens   string

What to do

1. Draw a large hand shape. To do this, lightly draw around your own hand and use this as a model to make a shape two or three times as large. On the hand write 'I can help'. Cut this out.

2. Draw five normal size hand shapes. On each one write a different way that you can use your hands to help others – at home, school, church or in the neighbourhood. Cut out these hand shapes.

3. Turn the hands into a mobile. Suspend the smaller hands from the thumb and fingers of the large hand.

4. Display the mobile in your room as a reminder to help other people.

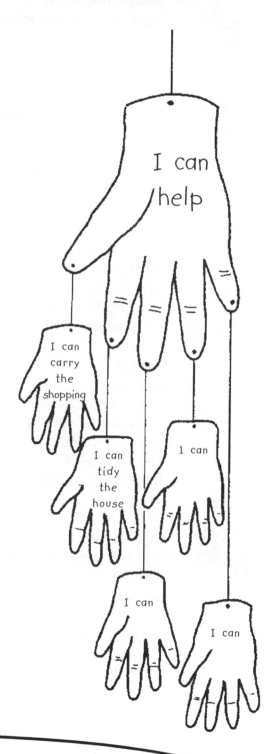

Jesus used his hands to heal.
We can use our hands to help.

This belongs to: . . . .

Helping hands

Today at church
Today at church we talked about how our hands can be used to help others. Then we heard how Jesus used his hands to heal the sick.

Gospel theme
Luke illustrates how Jesus healed the woman in the synagogue by placing his hands on her. Once again Jesus' work of healing brings him into controversy with the authorities, this time the leader of the synagogue.

Gospel passage (Luke 13.10-13)
Now Jesus was teaching in one of the synagogues on the sabbath.
And just then there appeared
a woman with a spirit that had crippled her for eighteen years.
She was bent over and was quite unable to stand up straight.
When Jesus saw her, he called her over and said,
'Woman, you are set free from your ailment.'
When he laid his hands on her,
immediately she stood up straight and began praising God.

Prayer
Lord Jesus Christ,
you laid your hands on the sick
and brought them healing.
Teach us to use our hands
that we may bring help to others;
for you are our God.
Amen.

Talking points
❖ our experiences of helping hands;
❖ the healing power of Jesus' hands;
❖ using our hands to help others.

Activity for younger children
Draw around your hand four or five times. In each shape draw a picture of ways you can use your hands to help others.

This belongs to: . . . .

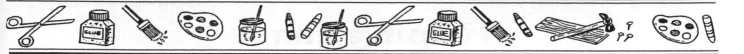

Make a turnaround mask

You will need

paper plate   pens, pencils or paint
scissors   elastic or ribbon

What to do

1. Make a mask that can be turned upside down to show a different expression. Held one way the mask will show a suffering face. Held the other way the mask will show a happy face. In our lives we have times of both happiness and suffering. Use the mask to remind yourself of this.
2. Copy the picture below onto your mask with pens, pencils or paints. Practise first on scrap paper. Remember that everything you draw must be part of the upside down picture. The lines in the forehead become the mouth when turned the other way around.
3. Cut out the eye holes, making sure they are in the correct position so you can see.
4. Attach elastic or ribbon so that you can wear the mask.

We all have times of suffering.
Jesus shared our suffering.

This belongs to: . . . .

Suffering

Today at church
Today at church we talked about our experiences of suffering. Then we heard how Jesus prepared to suffer on the cross.

Gospel theme
In Matthew's gospel Jesus gives explicit teaching about the kind of Messiah he really is. He is the Messiah who suffers alongside and on behalf of the people of God. Just as Peter found the idea of a suffering Messiah difficult to grasp, so have many future generations.

Gospel passage (Matthew 16.21-23)
From that time on,
Jesus began to show his disciples
that he must go to Jerusalem and undergo great suffering
at the hands of the elders and chief priests and scribes,
and be killed,
and on the third day be raised.
And Peter took him aside and began to rebuke him, saying,
'God forbid it, Lord!
This must never happen to you.'
But he turned and said to Peter,
'Get behind me, Satan!
You are a stumbling-block to me.'

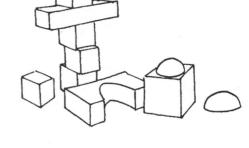

Prayer
Lord Jesus Christ,
you suffered for our sake.
Heal us by your suffering and death,
that we may share with you your risen life;
for you are our God.
Amen.

Talking points
❖　our experiences of suffering;
❖　suffering as a basic human experience;
❖　Jesus shared our suffering.

Activity for younger children
Make a card or a present to give to someone you know who is suffering, someone who is perhaps not well or perhaps upset.

This belongs to: . . . .

Keep a washing chart

Think

How many times a day do you wash part of yourself such as hands or teeth?
How many times a day does someone in your home wash dishes or clothes?
How often do you wash completely in a shower or bath? Washing is an
important part of our lives.

What to do

In the next week keep a record of all the times you wash yourself and all the
times that you or someone in the house washes articles that you use, such as
dishes or clothes or the floor.

My washing record			
	me	**dishes**	**clothes**
Monday			
Tuesday			
Wednesday			
Thursday			
Friday			
Saturday			
Sunday			

We keep our bodies and clothes clean.
Jesus said a clean heart is even more important.

This belongs to: . . . .

Washing

Today at church
Today at church we talked about how we wash our hands before eating. Then we heard how the Pharisees criticised Jesus for not keeping all the rituals and laws about washing.

Gospel theme
The Pharisees accuse Jesus of disregard for the ritual laws of washing. Jesus replies that a clean heart is more important than attention to the ritual laws of washing.

Gospel passage (Mark 7.1-3)
When the Pharisees and some of the scribes
who had come from Jerusalem gathered around Jesus,
they noticed that some of his disciples
were eating with defiled hands, that is, without washing them.
(For the Pharisees, and all the Jews,
do not eat unless they thoroughly wash their hands,
thus observing the tradition of the elders.)

Prayer
Lord Jesus Christ,
you call your people to
pure and holy lives.
Wash from us all that defiles
that we may serve you with clean hearts;
now and always.
Amen.

Talking points
❖ our experiences of washing for hygienic purposes;
❖ the Pharisees' concern with ritual washing;
❖ desiring inner cleanliness.

Activity for younger children
Conduct a soap search. Look around your home to collect all the things used for washing - for washing people, pets, clothes, dishes or cars. Make a display and show your family.

This belongs to: . . . .

Make a party pinata

You will need

balloon

flour or wallpaper paste

paint

string or ribbon

newspaper

scissors

wrapped sweets

tissue or crêpe paper

What to do

1. Blow up the balloon and tie a knot in the end.

2. Make paste (with the help of an adult) by heating 1 cup of flour and 3 cups of water until the mixture thickens. Allow it to cool before using it.

3. Tear up the newspaper into small pieces. Soak the pieces of paper in the paste and use them to cover the balloon. You need about five layers of paper. If you have coloured newspaper, paste on alternate layers of white and coloured paper, to make sure the layers are even. Leave this to dry thoroughly. This will take about two days.

4. Cut a hole (the size of an orange or apple) around the knot of the balloon. Cut two small holes either side. Thread the string or ribbon through the small holes to hang the pinata.

5. Paint the finished pinata. Fill it with sweets and lightly stuff the hole with tissue paper or crêpe paper.

6. Share the pinata with friends as a small party. Follow Jesus' advice and invite people who are not often invited to special times. Hang the pinata high. Take turns to hit it with a pole to shake out the sweets to share.

Jesus said to invite without thought of return. We can be generous with our party invitations.

This belongs to: . . . .

Party time

Today at church
Today at church we talked about the parties we have attended. Then we heard Jesus' teaching about how we should invite to our parties people who might not be able to invite us back.

Gospel theme
Jesus was invited to a meal in the house of a leader of the Pharisees. The purpose of offering hospitality, he argues, should not be the hope of hospitality returned, but the joy of selfless giving to those who are in no position to offer anything in return.

Gospel passage (Luke 14.12–14)
Jesus said also to the one who had invited him,
'When you give a luncheon or a dinner,
do not invite your friends or your brothers
or your relatives or rich neighbours,
in case they may invite you in return,
and you would be repaid.
But when you give a banquet,
invite the poor, the crippled, the lame, and the blind.
And you will be blessed, because they cannot repay you,
for you will be repaid at the resurrection of the righteous.'

Prayer
Lord Jesus Christ,
you invite all people to your table.
Give us generous hearts
that we may be open to the needs of others;
for you are our God.
Amen.

Talking points
❖ our experiences of parties;
❖ Jesus' criticism of the practice of his day;
❖ selfless hospitality.

Activity for younger children
Plan a party for your dolls and teddies. Invite some toys you have not played with recently. Plan music and party games for your toys.

This belongs to: . . . .

Make surprise cakes

You will need

125 g butter or margarine
1 teaspoon vanilla essence
250 g self raising flour
150 ml milk
cherries, nuts, sultanas, chocolate

190 g sugar
2 eggs
pinch salt
24 paper cake cases

What to do

1. Ask an adult to set the oven to 190°C (375°F or gas mark 5). Place the paper cake cases on a tray.
2. Cream the butter or margarine. Gradually add the sugar and beat the mixture until light and creamy. Add the vanilla.
3. Gently beat the eggs in a cup or bowl and add them to the mixture a small amount at a time, beating it well each time.
4. Gently fold the salt and some of the flour into the mixture, then some milk, repeating until it is all used up.
5. Spoon the mixture into the paper cases. In each cake place a surprise such as a cherry, nut, sultana or piece of chocolate.
6. Ask an adult to bake the cakes for about 15 minutes.
7. Serve the cakes as a game of hide and seek. Seek the special surprise in each cake.

We seek for lost items.
We are concerned for people who lose their way.

This belongs to: . . . .

Hide and seek

Today at church
Today at church we talked about how we like to play hide and seek. Then we heard about Jesus' concern for people who have lost their way.

Gospel theme
Matthew says that Christians have a responsibility to seek those who have lost their way, just as the Shepherd seeks the lost sheep. In the present passage Matthew sets down the method for doing so.

Gospel passage (Matthew 18.15–16)
Jesus said, 'If another member of the church sins against you,
go and point out the fault when the two of you are alone.
If the member listens to you,
you have regained that one.
But if you are not listened to,
take one or two others along with you,
so that every word may be confirmed
by the evidence of two or three witnesses.'

Prayer
Lord Jesus Christ,
you put right those who have lost their way.
Be gentle with us when we lose our way
and call us back to the right path,
that we may walk with you;
now and always.
Amen.

Talking points
❖ our experiences of hide and seek;
❖ the need to seek those who have lost their way;
❖ concern for all God's people.

Activity for younger children
Play a game of hide and seek with the family. Hide wrapped sweets, one or two for each person. Ask the family to find the sweets. They must work together to find them, then share them equally.

This belongs to: . . . .

Make a picture frame

You will need

heavy card
scissors
decorative objects

glue or tape
paper

What to do

1. Paint or draw a picture of a dog or find one from a magazine. Make a frame for the picture.
2. Cut out a large square or rectangle of cardboard (from a grocery box) with a hole the size of your picture. If you do not have a piece of cardboard large enough, cut out four strips of cardboard, and join them together.
3. Decorate the frame. Begin with strips of coloured paper or wrapping paper wound around the frame and glued at the back. If you want a three-dimensional effect, add objects such as paper straws, feathers and sequins.
4. Tape the picture in place in the frame. Display it in your room.

We show concern for our pets.
Jesus is concerned for all people.

This belongs to: . . . .

Dogs

Today at church
Today at church we talked about the different dogs we know. Then we heard the story from the Bible about how the dogs are allowed to eat the crumbs which fall from the table.

Gospel theme
Mark's gospel portrays Jesus conducting his ministry first among the Jewish people and then among the Gentiles. The Jewish people need to be fed first, but the turn of the Gentiles has now arrived. The Gentiles also deserve to be treated as God's children.

Gospel passage (Mark 7.25-28)
A woman whose little daughter had an unclean spirit
immediately heard about Jesus,
and she came and bowed down at his feet.
Now the woman was a Gentile,
of Syrophoenician origin.
She begged him to cast the demon out of her daughter.
He said to her,
'Let the children be fed first,
for it is not fair to take the children's food
and throw it to the dogs.'
But she answered him,
'Sir, even the dogs under the table eat the children's crumbs.'

Prayer
Lord Jesus Christ,
your love is for all people.
Teach us to share your love with all,
that your kingdom may reach
to the ends of the world;
for you are our God.
Amen.

Talking points
❖   our experiences of dogs;
❖   the significance of the children's food being given to the dogs;
❖   Jesus' concern is for everybody.

Activity for younger children
Make a kennel or basket for a toy dog. Use a cardboard box. Ask an adult to help you cut it to shape. Add a tea towel or piece of fabric as a blanket.

This belongs to: . . . .

Make a squirrel

You will need

fabric	scissors
needle	cotton
stuffing	glue

What to do

1. Draw a template of a squirrel like the one on this page but larger. Use it to cut out two pieces of fabric.
2. Sew the fabric pieces together, leaving a small hole at the bottom. Stuff the squirrel through the hole, then sew it up.
3. Make a line of stitches between the squirrel's body and its tail, sewing through the stuffing and pulling the stitches firmly.
4. Add features such as eyes by sewing or by gluing small pieces of fabric.

Squirrels plan ahead and prepare for winter.
We need to plan ahead before following Jesus.

This belongs to: . . . .

Squirrels

Today at church
Today at church we talked about how squirrels prepare for the winter by storing up nuts and food. Then we listened to Jesus' teaching about how we should prepare for proper discipleship.

Gospel theme
Jesus makes it clear that the disciples who continue with him on the journey need to show single-minded and determined commitment. They need to count the cost before setting out further on the road and decide whether they can complete the course.

Gospel passage (Luke 14.27–30)
Jesus said, 'Whoever does not carry the cross and follow me
cannot be my disciple.
For which of you,
intending to build a tower,
does not first sit down and estimate the cost,
to see whether he has enough to complete it?
Otherwise, when he has laid a foundation and is not able to finish,
all who see it will begin to ridicule him,
saying, "This fellow began to build and was not able to finish."'

Prayer
Lord Jesus Christ,
you teach your people
to count the cost of discipleship.
Give us grace to understand the cost
and to follow you in the way of the cross,
that we may be your true disciples;
now and always.
Amen.

Talking points
❖ our experiences of squirrels preparing for winter;
❖ Jesus' teaching about counting the cost;
❖ counting the cost and committing ourselves to discipleship.

Activity for younger children
Make a model of a squirrel from plasticine or playdough. Make nuts for the squirrel to collect and store.

This belongs to: . . . .

Keep a forgiveness record

Think

Peter thought he would be doing well if he forgave someone seven times. Jesus said that was not enough. He needed to forgive seventy-seven times, or even seventy multiplied by seven times. Jesus meant Peter was to keep on and on forgiving.

What to do

1. Keep a record for a week of the number of times you forgive someone, or the times you hear someone else forgiving. This forgiveness can be as simple as a reply such as 'That's okay' when someone says sorry.
2. At the end of a week, check your record and see how much forgiveness there is around. Is it anywhere near what Jesus said?

Monday	
Tuesday	
Wednesday	
Thursday	
Friday	
Saturday	
Sunday	

**Jesus said to keep on forgiving.
Forgiveness mends broken relationships.**

This belongs to: . . . .

Mender

Today at church
Today at church we talked about our experiences of people who mend and restore things. Then we listened to Jesus' teaching about how forgiveness mends relationships between people.

Gospel theme
Christians are people who have been forgiven much by God and should, therefore, go on showing forgiveness to others. To forgive is to mend and to restore relationships.

Gospel passage (Matthew 18.21-22)
Peter came and said to Jesus,
'Lord, if another member of the church sins against me,
how often should I forgive?
As many as seven times?'
Jesus said to him,
'Not seven times,
but, I tell you, seventy-seven times.'

Prayer
Lord Jesus Christ,
you call your followers
to be forgiving people.
Help us to forgive others
that we may live up to our calling;
for you are our God.
Amen.

Talking points
❖ our experiences of people who mend and restore things;
❖ forgiveness as mending relationships;
❖ being forgiving people.

Activity for younger children
Sort through your toys and books to find which ones need mending. Ask an adult to help you repair those which you can.

This belongs to: . . . .

Make a prayer montage

You will need

poster paper   newspapers

scissors   glue

What to do

1. There are many people in our world who feel hurt. Look through newspapers to find pictures, headlines and articles about hurt people. Cut them out.

2. Glue these items to a sheet of poster paper. Add to them the names of people you know who are hurt.

3. Display the montage in your room and use it as a focus for prayer. Each day pray for someone mentioned.

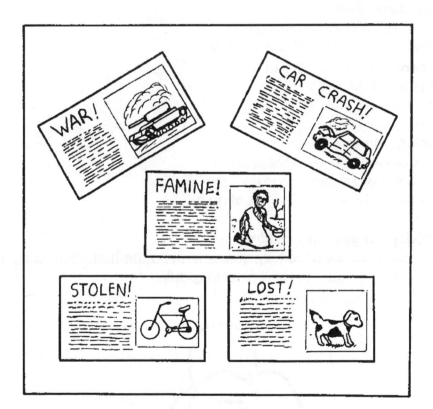

**We all feel hurt at some time.
Jesus shared our feelings of pain.**

This belongs to: . . . .

Feeling hurt

Today at church
Today at church we talked about the times when we feel hurt. Then we heard how Jesus was prepared to feel pain and hurt and to undergo great suffering.

Gospel theme
Jesus makes it plain to his disciples that he is not the warrior Messiah, whom some were expecting, but a fully human Messiah who is destined to suffer.

Gospel passage (Mark 8.31–32)
Then Jesus began to teach them
that the Son of Man must undergo great suffering,
and be rejected by the elders, the chief priests, and the scribes,
and be killed, and after three days rise again.
He said all this quite openly.

Prayer
Lord Jesus Christ,
you suffered pain for our sake.
Heal us by your suffering and death,
that we may share with you your risen life;
for you are our God.
Amen.

Talking points
❖   our experiences of feeling hurt;
❖   pain as a basic human experience;
❖   Jesus shared our feelings of pain.

Activity for younger children
Fill a box with things to help you when you are hurt. You could include plasters, tissues to dry your eyes and a toy to cuddle.

This belongs to: . . . .

Make a lost property noticeboard

You will need

cardboard   paper
scissors   glue

What to do

1. Cut out a large square or rectangle of cardboard (perhaps from a grocery box).
2. Cover the cardboard with bright paper. Glue on a border in a contrasting colour. Add the words 'Lost property'.
3. Put a pad of small Post-it stickers and a pen nearby, or else keep small sheets of paper and a pen in a box, along with Blu-tack to attach them to the board.
4. Display the board at home or at school (with your teacher's permission) and invite people to fill in notes when they lose items, and for others to check the board and help to find the lost items.

We worry about lost property.
God worries about lost people.

This belongs to: . . . .

Lost property

Today at church
Today at church we talked about our experiences of losing things. Then we listened to Jesus' story about the woman who lost a coin and went to great efforts to find it again.

Gospel theme
The welcome which Jesus extends to sinners causes the Pharisees and scribes to grumble. Jesus responds by telling parables to emphasise God's concern for the individual who is lost. The shepherd searches for the lost sheep. The woman searches for the lost coin.

Gospel passage (Luke 15.8–10)
Jesus said, 'What woman having ten silver coins,
if she loses one of them,
does not light a lamp, sweep the house,
and search carefully until she finds it?
When she has found it,
she calls together her friends and neighbours, saying,
"Rejoice with me,
for I have found the coin that I had lost."
Just so, I tell you,
there is joy in the presence of the angels of God
over one sinner who repents.'

Prayer
Lord Jesus Christ,
you rejoice when the lost are found.
We praise you for searching for us.
We praise you for finding us.
We praise you for keeping us safe
in your hands;
for you are our God.
Amen.

Talking points
❖   our experiences of lost property;
❖   God's concern for those who are lost;
❖   sharing God's search for those who are lost.

Activity for younger children
Make a necklace of coin rubbings. Place a coin under a sheet of paper and colour over it. Experiment to see how hard you need to press for the design to show through. Rub over ten coins, cut them out and glue them on a sheet of paper to make a picture of a necklace.

This belongs to: . . . .

Make awards

You will need

card   ribbon
pens

What to do

1. Each person in your family, and each person you know, deserves an award for something. Everyone is special. Make a list of people and one thing for which each person is special. Be sure not to miss anyone out. If you choose people from your class at school, then include the whole class.
2. Make simple awards for each person. Cut circles from card. Glue or staple ribbons or strips of fabric or paper to the bottom.
3. Write on each award. You could write 'For a special person' on every award or you could write a personal message on each, such as 'For Gary, a fast runner' or 'For Sian, a great friend'.
4. Choose a good time to hand out your awards.

In Jesus' story, all the workers were rewarded.
We can plan awards for all of our group.

This belongs to: . . . .

Prizes for all

Today at church
Today at church we talked about those games in which everyone receives prizes. Then we heard Jesus' story about the landowner who gave equal wages to those who worked all day and to those who started late in the day.

Gospel theme
The parable of the labourers in the vineyard makes the point that God rewards all equally, at whatever point they responded to the call of the kingdom. Latecomers are entitled to the same reward as those who have borne the burden of the day. Tax collectors are as welcome as Pharisees.

Gospel passage (Matthew 20.8-10)
Jesus said, 'When evening came, the owner of the vineyard said to his manager, "Call the labourers and give them their pay, beginning with the last and then going to the first."'
When those hired about five o'clock came, each of them received the usual daily wage.
Now when the first came, they thought they would receive more; but each of them also received the usual daily wage.'

Prayer
Lord Jesus Christ,
you welcome all your people
into your kingdom.
Give us grace to love you,
that we may use our lives in your service;
for you are our God.
Amen.

Talking points
❖ our experiences of games in which all receive equal prizes;
❖ the value of games for their own sake not for the prize;
❖ the values of the kingdom of heaven.

Activity for younger children
Make a model of a silver cup for each person in your family. Use paper cups or plastic cups. Cover them with cooking foil.

This belongs to: . . . .

Make a learning chart

Think

Jesus said to welcome children. Adults say that we can learn a lot from children if we listen carefully. Have you ever listened to what younger children say to see what you can learn from them?

What to do

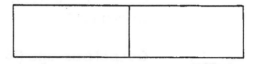

1. Join together two sheets of A4 paper. Fold them fanwise into about eight sections. Cut about 5 cm off the top to make the proportion more like a human figure.

2. On the top fold, draw an outline of a child, making sure that feet and hands touch the joins. Cut this out, cutting through all the sections. Be careful not to cut along the folds where the feet and hands join. You should have a string of eight figures joined together.

3. Display your string of figures. During the week listen carefully to what younger children say. When you hear an important message (such as about friendship or caring for others) write it on one of the figures, perhaps with the name of the child who said it. Even when the string of figures is filled up, continue listening to children for what you can learn.

Jesus said to welcome children in his name.
We can learn by listening to children.

This belongs to: . . . .

Children

Today at church
Today at church we talked about what it is like to be children. Children are small and less powerful than adults. Then we heard Jesus tell his disciples that they should not want to be powerful.

Gospel theme
Jesus has explained to his disciples that he will suffer. This view of Messiahship reverses the common expectation for a triumphal Messiah. Such a reversal must change the disciples' hopes for themselves as well. In place of power they find weakness.

Gospel passage (Mark 9.33-36)
Then they came to Capernaum;
and when he was in the house he asked them,
'What were you arguing about on the way?'
But they were silent,
for on the way they had argued with one another
who was the greatest.
He sat down, called the twelve, and said to them,
'Whoever wants to be first
must be last of all and servant of all.'
Then he took a little child and put it among them.

Prayer
Lord Jesus Christ,
you call your followers
to give service to others
and not to seek power for themselves.
Help us to live up to our calling,
that our lives may witness to you;
now and always.
Amen.

Talking points
❖ our experiences of childhood;
❖ the powerlessness of children;
❖ Jesus reverses expectations of power.

Activity for younger children
Jesus said to welcome children. Spend an hour playing with a younger child, doing what that child wants. (If you are always the youngest, then persuade an older person to play with you for an hour, doing what you want.)

This belongs to: . . . .

Make a crossroads sign

You will need

card   scissors

pens

What to do

1. Cut out two rectangles of card the same size and shape. In the middle of each long side, cut a slit to halfway. Slot these two pieces together to make a crossroads sign.

2. At a crossroads we need to make a decision about which road to take. The directions on the sign help us to choose. In life we often need to make choices about what to do. Write directions or questions on the crossroad sign to help you make the best choice. Some questions could be:

    Would it hurt others?
    Would it help others?
    Would it make me happy?
    Would Jesus agree?
    Does it cost money?
    Do I have the time?
    Do I need help from others?

3. Each time you need to make a decision, try out your questions on each choice to help you find the best one.

**We need to make wise choices.
Jesus encourages us to choose to live his way.**

This belongs to: . . . .

Crossroads

Today at church
Today at church we talked about crossroads and how we have to make choices at crossroads. Then we heard Jesus' teaching about how we have to choose to follow him.

Gospel theme
Jesus presents us with a choice and with the need to make a decision. We cannot be half-hearted disciples. We need to choose.

Gospel passage (Luke 16.13)
Jesus said, 'No slave can serve two masters;
for a slave will either hate the one and love the other,
or be devoted to the one and despise the other.
You cannot serve God and wealth.'

Prayer
Lord Jesus Christ,
you call your people
to choose your way.
Help us to follow you
with all our being,
that we may be called your people;
for you are our God.
Amen.

Talking points
❖ our experiences of crossroads;
❖ the choice which Jesus presents;
❖ choosing Jesus' way.

Activity for younger children
Paint a picture of a crossroads near you. Add in what you would find if you travelled down each road, for example school, church, shops, park, friend's house.

This belongs to: . . . .

Play a game

What to do

- Place a counter for each player on 'start'. Take turns throwing a die and moving your counter the number of squares shown.
- If you land on a 'trap' square, follow the instructions given.
- The winner is the first person to reach 'home'.

start		trap miss a turn		
				trap go back to start
	trap go back 5 spaces			
trap go back 3 spaces				
		trap miss a turn		home

We experience traps in games.
The Jewish authorities set traps for Jesus.

This belongs to: . . . .

Setting traps

Today at church
Today at church we talked about how traps can be set for us to fall into. Then we heard how people had set traps and trick questions to catch Jesus out.

Gospel theme
Immediately prior to this conversation, Jesus has ridden into Jerusalem on a donkey and been greeted with shouts of 'Hosanna'. Now the Jewish authorities want to trap Jesus into speaking out the claims of Messiahship portrayed by such actions. Jesus refuses to fall into this trap and sets one of his own.

Gospel passage (Matthew 21.23-25)
When Jesus entered the temple,
the chief priests and the elders of the people came to him as he was teaching,
and said, 'By what authority are you doing these things,
and who gave you this authority?'
Jesus said to them,
'I will also ask you one question;
if you tell me the answer,
then I will also tell you by what authority I do these things.
Did the baptism of John come from heaven,
or was it of human origin?'

Prayer
Lord Jesus Christ,
you made sound judgements
and were blameless before your accusers.
Give us a sound sense of judgement,
that we may witness to you
in confidence and in truth;
for you are our God.
Amen.

Talking points
❖ our experiences of setting traps;
❖ the traps set for Jesus;
❖ how Jesus dealt with such traps.

Activity for younger children
Play a game with other members of your family. Make sure that all agree. Take turns to set *safe* traps for each other, traps such as jumping out and shouting 'Boo!' as people pass.

This belongs to: . . . .

Make a book

You will need

card	scissors or craft knife
decorative paper	glue
A4 paper	hole punch
strong cord	pens or pencils

What to do

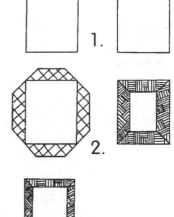

1. Cut two pieces of thick card that are about 1 cm wider and longer than an A4 page.

2. Cut out two sheets of decorative paper (such as wallpaper) that are about 5 cm wider and longer than A4 (about 4 cm larger than the card). Glue the sheets of card to the paper, cutting the edges as in the diagram and folding them over. Glue them to the back.

3. Glue a sheet of plain paper to the back of each cover to hide the edges of the paper. Choose paper in a colour that goes well with the cover paper.

4. Lay a sheet of A4 paper in the centre of each cover and mark where the holes go. Punch them through with a hole punch.

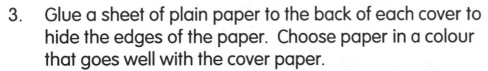

5. Place sheets of A4 paper on the back cover, lining up the holes, then put the front cover on top. Thread a strong, decorative cord through the holes and finish with a knot or bow.

6. Use your book to keep a record of Jesus' gang. Use this as your title. Keep a new page for each group you hear of that works in Jesus' name. This could be a missionary group, a shelter for homeless people, a church youth group and many more. Write the date you heard of the group, the job it does, where it works and any other information. Keep this book as a record of the work that people do in Jesus' name.

> **Gangs work and play together.**
> **Jesus' gang works to help others in his name.**

This belongs to: . . . .

Gangs

Today at church
Today at church we talked about how children form gangs and how they exclude others from their gang. Then we heard how Jesus refused to exclude others from working in his name.

Gospel theme
Jesus affirms the exorcist who casts out demons in his name, even though this exorcist is working independently of the close band of followers. The church, like Jesus, must be willing to recognise the activity of God in a wider context.

Gospel passage (Mark 9.38-40)
John said to him,
'Teacher, we saw someone casting out demons in your name,
and we tried to stop him, because he was not following us.'
But Jesus said, 'Do not stop him;
for no one who does a deed of power in my name
will be able soon afterwards to speak evil of me.
Whoever is not against us is for us.'

Prayer
Lord Jesus Christ,
you welcomed all who worked through your name.
Help us to work with your followers
from other churches and other traditions,
that your kingdom may grow;
now and always.
Amen.

Talking points
❖ our experiences of gangs;
❖ Jesus refused to exclude people working in his name;
❖ the power of Jesus working through unexpected people.

Activity for younger children
Make your own 'gang' from paper. Join together two sheets of paper to make a long strip. Ask an adult to help you fold it fanwise into eight sections. On the top section draw a person with the arms and legs extending to the edges. Cut this out so that you have a long string of people. Colour them in.

This belongs to: . . . .

Help the needy

Think

People are needy in many different ways. Here are four areas of need. Do you know any people like this? Can you and your family help? Can you think of any other needy people?

The poor

There are poor people in our country and in other lands. There are charities to help. You could save small coins to give. You and your friends could hold a stall or put on a concert to raise money.

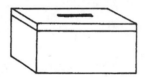

Those with few clothes

Sort out good clothes that no longer fit you and your family. Give them to a family you know or phone the council to see if there are any local groups that can use these clothes.

The hungry

Collect tins of food to give to a local shelter for the homeless, or pack a lunch to give to a hungry person you have seen begging on the streets.

The upset

When you see someone crying or upset, offer help and comfort. If a child is upset and has no one to play with, invite him or her to play with you. If someone has been injured, get help.

There are people in need all around us. We can help care for them.

This belongs to: . . . .

The needy

Today at church
Today at church we talked about people who are in need. Then we listened to Jesus' story about the rich man and the poor man called Lazarus.

Gospel theme
Here is a parable which contrasts the experiences of the poor man (Lazarus) and the rich man. Lazarus longed to satisfy his hunger with what fell from the rich man's table. The parable ends by painting a graphic picture of the consequences of ignoring the needs of the poor.

Gospel passage (Luke 16.19–22)
Jesus said, 'There was a rich man who was dressed in purple and fine linen and who feasted sumptuously every day.
And at his gate lay a poor man named Lazarus, covered with sores,
who longed to satisfy his hunger
with what fell from the rich man's table;
even the dogs would come and lick his sores.
The poor man died
and was carried away by the angels to be with Abraham.
The rich man also died and was buried.'

Prayer
Lord Jesus Christ,
you uphold the cause of the poor.
Strengthen your people today,
that we may stand alongside the poor;
to your praise and glory.
Amen.

Talking points
❖ our experiences of the needy;
❖ the parable to care for the needy;
❖ our commitment to the needs of others.

Activity for younger children
There are many people in need in this country and in the world. Make a money box to collect small coins to help. This could be a small plastic tub with a hole cut in the lid, decorated to look attractive. Ask members of your family to put in any pennies they get as change. When the box is full, give the money to a charity that helps those in need.

This belongs to: . . . .

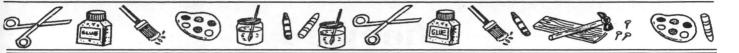

Make a bookmark

You will need

    white card   pens
    scissors

What to do

1.   On a sheet of white card, draw a bunch of grapes, or copy the picture below. Colour it. Cut it out.
2.   On the back write a message such as 'I choose to serve God.'
3.   Cut two slits as shown. Use it as a bookmark by placing the middle section over the page you are using, and the two outer sections behind.

I choose to serve God

The vineyard is a picture of God's people.
We can choose to serve God.

This belongs to: . . . .

Vineyard

Today at church
Today at church we talked about vineyards and the places where grapes are grown and wine is made. Then we listened to Jesus' story about the bad tenants who were disloyal to the owner of the vineyard.

Gospel theme
The parable of the vineyard spells out how the tenants had killed the owner's son. Then it invites the listeners to pass judgement on the tenants in the story. In so doing the listeners pass judgement on themselves. God will entrust the vineyard to others.

Gospel passage (Matthew 21.33–35)
Jesus said, 'Listen to another parable.
There was a landowner who planted a vineyard,
put a fence around it, dug a wine press in it,
and built a watch-tower.
Then he leased it to tenants and went to another country.
When the harvest time had come,
he sent his slaves to the tenants to collect his produce.
But the tenants seized his slaves
and beat one, killed another, and stoned another.'

Prayer
Lord Jesus Christ,
you call us to work in your vineyard.
Make us worthy of our calling,
that we may grow good fruit for you;
now and always.
Amen.

Talking points
❖ our experiences and images of vineyards;
❖ the vineyard in the Bible;
❖ serving God as good tenants in the vineyard.

Activity for younger children
Make a collage picture of a bunch of grapes. Draw the outline, then screw up coloured paper (tissue paper or crêpe paper are best) into balls for each grape and glue it to the bunch. Add green paper leaves.

This belongs to: . . . .

Make a bridal party

You will need

cardboard cylinders   paper
paper doily   scissors
glue   cotton balls
pens   wool

What to do

1. Find cardboard cylinders. These can be from cling film rolls or toilet paper or anything similar. Cut larger rolls to about the size of toilet rolls.

2. Make a bride. Cut a triangular piece out of a lace doily. Join the larger piece as a cone for the wedding dress, slitting and tucking the centre to the inside of the cylinder to hold it in place. Glue on a cotton wool ball or a polystyrene ball as a head. Draw on a face. Glue on wool for hair. Use the small triangular section as a veil. Arms can be added with pipe cleaners or straws.

3. Make a groom. Glue dark paper around a cylinder. Glue on a small triangle of white for the shirt, along with a coloured section as a tie. Add a head and arms.

4. Make other members of the bridal party in the same way.

A wedding is a special time.
We celebrate.

This belongs to: . . . .

Wedding service

Today at church
Today at church we talked about wedding services and about getting married. Then we listened to Jesus' teaching on divorce.

Gospel theme
Jesus' teaching about divorce is presented somewhat differently by Matthew and Mark. In Mark Jesus is asked the question, 'Is it lawful for a man to divorce his wife?' Matthew adds to this question the words 'for any cause'. In Jewish circles the debate was not about whether divorce was legal, but the grounds on which it was legal. And so the debate has continued in the Christian church.

Gospel passage (Mark 10.6-9)
Jesus said, 'From the beginning of creation,
"God made them male and female."
"For this reason a man shall leave his father and mother
and be joined to his wife,
and the two shall become one flesh."
So they are no longer two, but one flesh.
Therefore what God has joined together, let no one separate.'

Prayer
Lord Jesus Christ,
you taught your followers
the way of family life.
Bless parents and children
that their lives may reflect your praise;
now and always.
Amen.

Talking points
❖   our experiences of wedding services;
❖   the ideals of Christian marriages;
❖   Christian views on divorce.

Activity for younger children
Make a collage picture of a bride and groom. Cut out a paper doily for the bride's dress and veil. Use dark paper for the groom. Add wool for the hair.

This belongs to: . . . .

Keep a traveller's map

You will need

atlas or maps   paper
pens and pencils

What to do

1. We all travel to many different places. Sometimes it is places close to home. Sometimes it is places within the United Kingdom. Sometimes it is places around the world. Think of where you have been.

2. If your travels have been around the world, trace a map of the world from an atlas. If your travels have been around the United Kingdom, trace a map of this from an atlas or road map. If your travels have been local, use a local map and trace your area.

3. Mark in the places to which you have travelled. You can do this by drawing a line from your home to these places, or by attaching a length of ribbon, or by colouring in the places you have been.

4. Display your map and add to it each time you travel somewhere new.

Following Jesus is a journey of life.
We need to keep travelling.

This belongs to: . . . .

Journeys

Today at church
Today at church we talked about some of the journeys we have made. Following Jesus is like going on a journey. Then we listened to Jesus' teaching about discipleship.

Gospel theme
As Jesus draws still closer to Jerusalem in Luke's gospel, he continues to instruct his followers in the way of discipleship. All that we can offer is less than God deserves.

Gospel passage (Luke 17.7-10)
Jesus said, 'Who among you would say to your slave
who has just come in from ploughing or tending sheep in the field,
"Come here at once and take your place at the table"?
Would you not rather say to him,
"Prepare supper for me,
put on your apron and serve me while I eat and drink;
later you may eat and drink"?
Do you thank the slave for doing what was commanded?
So you also,
when you have done all that you were ordered to do, say,
"We are worthless slaves;
we have done only what we ought to have done!"'

Prayer
Lord Jesus Christ,
you have called us
to follow in your footsteps.
Give us joy in following you,
that we ask for no reward
other than that of doing your will;
for you are our God.
Amen.

Talking points
❖   our experiences of journeys;
❖   discipleship as a journey;
❖   persevering on the journey of discipleship.

Activity for younger children
Plan a journey for some of your toys. Pack a bag with things they will need. Make a cardboard boat or plane or car in which the toys can travel. Set off. Your journey could be around your house or garden, stopping at imaginary places.

This belongs to: . . . .

Make a birthday invitation

You will need

paper   ruler

pens   scissors

What to do

1. First, make a practice tri-tetraflexagon. Carefully copy the shape below. If you use A4 paper, rule squares of 5 cm. Number the squares as shown. The shaded squares are the front and the plain squares are the back.

2. With the front facing you, fold the top left two squares back and the bottom right square forward so that all the number twos are in front and the number ones are at the back. Join two edges with sticky tape as shown.

3. To flex the structure, fold it back vertically along the centre. Open up and you will find side three.

4. Use this pattern to make birthday invitations. Instead of writing numbers, write information. Face 1 could give your name and the name of the person you are inviting. Face 2 could give the date. Face 3 could give the address.

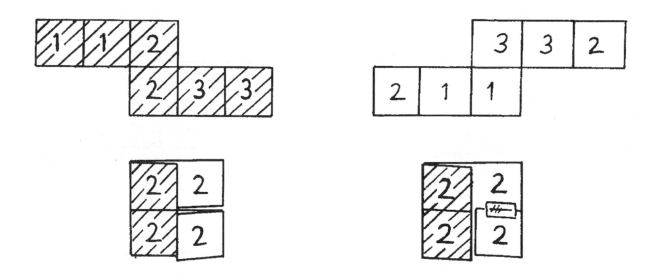

We invite friends to special occasions.
Jesus invites us to join him.

This belongs to: . . . .

Birthday invitations

Today at church
Today at church we talked about invitations we have received to birthday parties. Then we listened to Jesus' teaching about the king who invited people to a wedding banquet for his son and about how they refused to come.

Gospel theme
Through the imagery of the Old Testament, the wedding feast had become an established symbol for the age of the Messiah. This parable spells out how the people originally invited (the people of Israel) had declined the invitation. Therefore, God will invite others to the table.

Gospel passage (Matthew 22.1-5)
Once more Jesus spoke to the chief priests and Pharisees in parables, saying:
The kingdom of heaven may be compared to a king
who gave a wedding banquet for his son.
He sent his slaves to call those
who had been invited to the wedding banquet,
but they would not come.
Again he sent other slaves, saying,
"Tell those who have been invited:
Look, I have prepared my dinner,
my oxen and my fat calves have been slaughtered,
and everything is ready;
come to the wedding banquet."
But they made light of it and went away.'

Prayer
Lord Jesus Christ,
you invite us to your table.
Give us grace to accept your invitation,
that we may sit and eat with you in your kingdom;
for you are our God.
Amen.

Talking points
❖ our experiences of birthday invitations;
❖ the invitation to the wedding banquet;
❖ accepting the invitation offered to us.

Activity for younger children
Plan a birthday party for one of your toys. Make invitations to give to the other toys to attend.

This belongs to: . . . .

Make a list

You will need

paper   pens
boxes

What to do

1. Do you know all the things you own? Make a list to see how many possessions you actually have. Make one list for books and another list for toys. As you work through them, sort out your toys and perhaps put them into boxes. Use one box for soft toys, one for cars, one for board games, one for action toys and so on.

2. Jesus warned his followers that the things we own can sometimes become too important to us and take over our lives. How important are your possessions to you? Now that you have sorted them, are there any that you no longer need and could give away to a brother or sister or to a younger friend?

3. See which possessions mean the most to you. Ask a parent to look after one box of toys for you for a week. How much did you miss it? The next week take back that box and put away another box. Perhaps try one week without the television. Which things did you miss most? Do any of them take over your life?

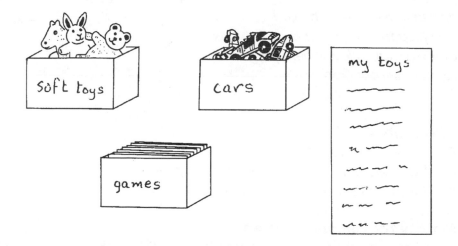

We own many things.
Jesus is more important than any of these.

This belongs to: . . . .

Possessions

Today at church
Today at church we talked about our possessions and how possessions can sometimes become too important to us. Then we heard how Jesus told the young man to get rid of his possessions before following him.

Gospel theme
Jesus' teaching on discipleship draws a stark contrast between those who have left everything to follow him and those who have kept their hearts fixed on the alternative goal of human possessions and wealth.

Gospel passage (Mark 10.17, 21–22)
As Jesus was setting out on a journey,
a man ran up and knelt before him, and asked him,
'Good Teacher, what must I do to inherit eternal life?'
Jesus, looking at him, loved him and said,
'You lack one thing; go, sell what you own,
and give the money to the poor,
and you will have treasure in heaven;
then come, follow me.'
When he heard this,
he was shocked and went away grieving,
for he had many possessions.

Prayer
Lord Jesus Christ,
you call us to follow you
and to leave all else behind.
Teach us to love you above all things,
that we may follow where you lead;
for you are our God.
Amen.

Talking points
❖ our experiences of possessions;
❖ how possessions take over people's lives;
❖ giving Jesus priority over possessions.

Activity for younger children
Look through catalogues. Cut out pictures of all the things you own. Glue these to a sheet of paper. At the top write 'Thank you for all of these.' At the bottom write 'Thank you for Jesus.'

This belongs to: . . . .

Print thank you cards

You will need

wooden block
string
glue
paper

pencil
scissors
paints

What to do

1. Find a smooth block of wood. On it write the words 'Thank you' in reverse writing as below. To check that you have got it right, hold your block up to the mirror. The letters should come out correctly.
2. Glue thick string over the shapes of the letters to make a printing block. If you wish you could also glue string in a decorative pattern around the outside. Leave the glue to dry.
3. Dip the painting block in paint, or paint over the string. Carefully press the block onto paper to print the words. Practise to see how hard you need to press so that you only print the words and not the background.
4. Use this block to print thank you cards to send to people you know. You can thank people for being your friend or for things they have done to help you. Keep a supply of cards at home to use at any time you wish.

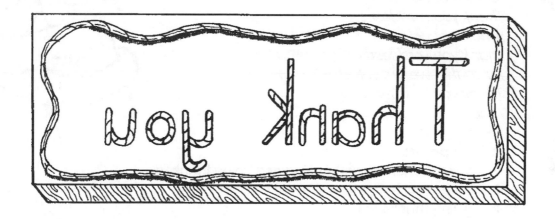

It is good to say thank you.
We can thank God.

This belongs to: . . . .

Thank you

Today at church
Today at church we talked about how we say thank you to other people and how they say thank you to us. Then we heard how Jesus cured ten lepers and how only one returned to say thank you.

Gospel theme
As Jesus now draws close to Jerusalem in Luke's gospel, he is met by ten lepers. All ten lepers were healed, but just one returned to thank Jesus. This man was a Samaritan, a foreigner.

Gospel passage (Luke 17.12-16)
As Jesus entered a village,
ten lepers approached him.
Keeping their distance,
they called out, saying,
'Jesus, Master, have mercy on us!'
When he saw them, he said to them,
'Go and show yourselves to the priests.'
And as they went, they were made clean.
Then one of them, when he saw that he was healed,
turned back, praising God with a loud voice.
He prostrated himself at Jesus' feet and thanked him.

Prayer
Thank you Lord Jesus,
for all that we are.
Thank you Lord Jesus,
for all that we have.
Thank you Lord Jesus,
for all that we are called to become.
Thank you Lord Jesus.
Amen.

Talking points
❖ our experiences of thanking and being thanked;
❖ Luke's teaching about the healed leper;
❖ giving thanks to God.

Activity for younger children
Make thank you cards to give to people you know. Keep a supply in your room to hand out whenever someone helps you or does something special for you.

This belongs to: . . . .

Make a coin collection box

You will need

box   cardboard strips
scissors   glue
fabric

What to do

1. Begin to collect coins from other countries. You will need a box in which to display them, a box with a separate section for each coin.

2. Find a suitable box. It does not have to be deep. Cut several strips of cardboard as long as the box, and more as wide as the box. They only need to be about 4 cm high. Fold them in half lengthways.

3. Measure the largest coin you have. The sections in your box will need to be that size. Cut slits to the centre lines of the cardboard strips that distance apart.

4. Slot the strips together. The slits for the length should all be facing down while the strips for the width all face up. Keep the fold in place so that half of each strip is upright and half can be glued into the box. Glue or staple the sections where the strips meet.

5. Glue the partitions into the box. Place a small piece of fabric in each partition to display the coins well.

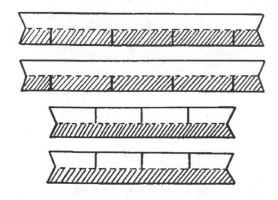 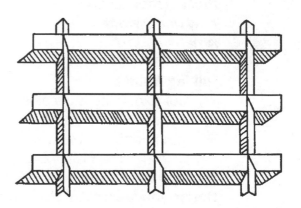

> **Our coins show respect for our country's leaders.**
> **Our lives show worship for God.**

This belongs to: . . . .

Coins

Today at church
Today at church we talked about coins and bank notes. We looked at the pictures and writing on them. Then we listened to Jesus' teaching about taxes.

Gospel theme
The final round of conflict between Jesus and the Jewish authorities before the Passion Narrative is presented in terms of three test questions. The question about paying taxes was to test whether Jesus sided with the zealots who refused to pay, or with those who collaborate with the Romans.

Gospel passage (Matthew 22.19-21)
Jesus said, 'Show me the coin used for the tax.'
And they brought him a denarius.
Then he said to them,
'Whose head is this, and whose title?'
They answered, 'The emperor's.'
Then he said to them,
'Give therefore to the emperor the things that are the emperor's,
and to God the things that are God's.'

Prayer
Lord Jesus Christ,
you taught your followers
to be good citizens and loyal servants of God.
Teach us to give proper attention
to the demands of society and the laws of God,
that we may be true citizens of your kingdom;
now and always.
Amen.

Talking points
❖ our experiences of coins;
❖ appropriate respect for civil authorities;
❖ giving appropriate worship to God.

Activity for younger children
Design your own set of coins. Look at coins from this country and any you may have from holidays to see how coins are designed. Plan your own, perhaps with a picture of a different person from your family on each coin.

This belongs to: . . . .

Make a badge

You will need

paper
card
safety pins

pens
scissors
tape

What to do

1. Jesus said that he came to serve others. He said that his followers must do the same. Make a list of people you know who serve God by serving other people. This can include those who look after a sick neighbour, those who clean the church, those who comfort people who are sad, and many more.

2. On scrap paper, design a badge for these people. Write words such as 'God's servant'. Plan your own 'servant' logo with items such as a broom or pen or plate of food.

3. Make badges with this logo. Cut out circles of card (or other shapes if you consider these more suitable). Draw your design. On the back, tape a safety pin so the badge can be worn.

4. Give or send your badges to people who you consider work for others as servants of God.

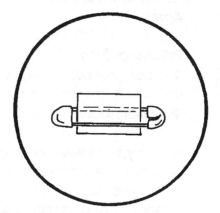

**Jesus came to serve us.
We can share his work by serving others.**

This belongs to: . . . .

Servant

Today at church
Today at church we talked about the service other people give to us and the service we can give to them. Then we heard how Jesus came not to be served, but to serve.

Gospel theme
The third prediction of Jesus' passion and death given by Mark is followed by this request from James and John to be given special status alongside the Messiah. Jesus replies that he came not to be served but to serve. The disciples must learn from his example.

Gospel passage (Mark 10.43–45)
Jesus said, 'Whoever wishes to become great among you must be your servant, and whoever wishes to be first among you must be slave of all.
For the Son of Man came not to be served but to serve,
and to give his life a ransom for many.'

Prayer
Lord Jesus Christ,
you came not to be served,
but to be servant of all.
Inspire us to follow your example
of service to others,
that we in turn may welcome
your service to us;
for you are our God.
Amen.

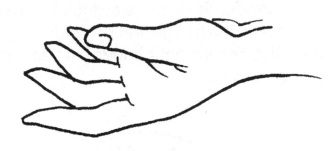

Talking points
❖ our experiences of servants;
❖ Jesus' emphasis on service;
❖ sharing Jesus' attitude of service.

Activity for younger children
Design a uniform for a 'servant of God', one who serves God by helping other people. This is a proud job so design a proud, bright uniform. You could make special armbands or a special cap.

This belongs to: . . . .

Compare the seasons

You will need

paper   pens
paint

What to do

1. Compare plants at different times of the year. Choose three plants in your garden or in a local park to visit once each season for the next year.

2. Each season sketch these three plants. Make sketches from a distance and from close up. Date each sketch (If you wish, you could also take photographs.) At the end of the year you will have four pictures. Compare these pictures. Look for differences between autumn and the other seasons.

3. Each season collect a few leaves from the bushes (or a twig in winter). Press these leaves between sheets of brown paper under a heavy book. Compare the leaves at the end of the year. In what way are autumn leaves different?

4. Make leaf prints for each season. Collect a few leaves, paint over one side and press it onto paper to get the pattern of the leaves. At the end of the year compare the size and condition of the prints.

Autumn leaves remind us of spring growth to come. God's promises give us hope for each day.

This belongs to: . . . .

Autumn days

Today at church
Today at church we talked about Autumn days. We looked at how the trees have lost their leaves and yet show promise of new growth in the Spring. We heard Jesus' teaching that we can trust God's promises.

Gospel theme
Jesus teaches that God listens to the people of God who pray day and night. We should not give up hope simply because there seems to be no immediate answer to prayer. In this sense the Christian is exhorted to go on praying for God's will to be done.

Gospel passage (Luke 18.1, 7-8)
Jesus told his disciples a parable about their need to pray always
and not to lose heart.
He said, 'Will not God grant justice to his chosen ones
who cry to him day and night?
Will he delay long in helping them?
I tell you, he will quickly grant justice to them.'

Prayer
Lord Jesus Christ,
your promises can be truly trusted.
Open our eyes to the promises
of your kingdom all around us,
that we may place
our full trust and confidence in you;
now and always.
Amen.

Talking points
❖   our experiences of autumn;
❖   seeing signs of spring through the autumn sign of death;
❖   trusting God's promises.

Activity for younger children
Make a 'feely box' containing conkers and nuts and seedpods and other special autumn items. Decorate a box to hold these special items. Display the box in your room to look at. Close your eyes and feel the special shapes.

This belongs to: . . . .

Make a heart mobile

You will need

wire coat hanger   raffia or coloured paper strips
coloured card

What to do

1. Bend a wire coat hanger into a heart shape, keeping the hook of the hanger pointing down. Ask an adult to cut off the hook.
2. Cover the heart with raffia or with strips of coloured paper wound round and round.
3. Cut a smaller heart shape from coloured card. Onto this, glue a photo of someone who makes you feel loved. Punch a hole in the top and thread it with string. Suspend this smaller heart from the raffia covered one.
4. Suspend the heart mobile in your room.

**Many people make us feel loved.
Jesus said that love is important.**

This belongs to: . . . .

Feeling loved

Today at church
Today at church we talked about our experiences of feeling loved. Then we listened to the two great commandments - to love God and to love our neighbours.

Gospel theme
When Jesus was asked to identify the greatest commandment, he cited two texts from the Old Testament. This answer sums up the centrality of love within the Christian gospel: love for God and love for others.

Gospel passage (Matthew 22.37-40)
Jesus said, '"You shall love the Lord your God with all your heart,
and with all your soul, and with all your mind."
This is the greatest and first commandment.
And a second is like it:
"You shall love your neighbour as yourself."
On these two commandments hang all the law and the prophets.'

Prayer
Lord Jesus Christ,
you show unfailing love to your people.
Teach us to love you
with all our heart,
with all our soul,
and with all our mind,
that we may walk with you
all the days of our lives;
through Jesus Christ our Lord.
Amen.

Talking points
* ❖ our experiences of feeling loved;
* ❖ the nature of Christian love;
* ❖ living the Christian life of love.

Activity for younger children
Cut out a large heart shape from red paper (or from white paper and colour it red). Glue this to cardboard to make it strong. On the heart glue a photograph of someone who makes you feel loved. Display the heart in your room.

This belongs to: . . . .

Make a blindfold

You will need

fabric   scissors
elastic   needle
thread

What to do

1. Cut out fabric pieces the size and shape below. Choose dark fabric if possible. Experiment, holding them over your eyes to see if they are thick enough to block out light.

2. If you do not have any thick fabric, then sew several pieces together, overstitching around the outside.

3. Sew a length of elastic to one end of the blindfold. Hold the blindfold over your face to check how long the elastic needs to be to fit your head snugly. Cut it to size and sew it in place.

4. Use the blindfold in games or to experience how it feels to be blind. Try walking around the house blindfolded. Sit in front of the television to see how much you can understand just by sound. Wear the blindfold for an hour and see how your life is affected.

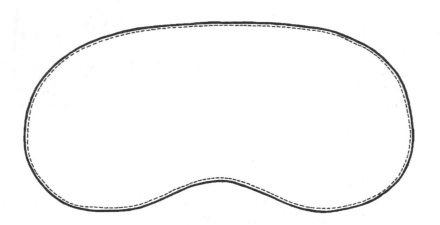

Jesus healed a blind beggar.
We thank God for our sight.

This belongs to: . . . .

Blindness

Today at church
Today at church we talked about the experience of being blind, about sight and about insight. Then we heard how the blind man Bartimaeus had real insight into who Jesus was.

Gospel theme
At Caesarea Philippi Peter confessed Jesus as Messiah for the first time. Since then Jesus has been reshaping the disciples' understanding of Messiahship, although they have found this teaching difficult to grasp. But now even the blind man sees Jesus for who he really is and, as a consequence, his blindness is healed.

Gospel passage (Mark 10.46–47, 51–52)
As Jesus and his disciples and a large crowd were leaving Jericho,
Bartimaeus son of Timaeus, a blind beggar,
was sitting by the roadside.
When he heard that it was Jesus of Nazareth,
he began to shout out and say,
'Jesus, Son of David, have mercy on me!'
Then Jesus said to him,
'What do you want me to do for you?'
The blind man said to him,
'My teacher, let me see again.'
Jesus said to him,
'Go; your faith has made you well.'

Prayer
Lord Jesus Christ,
you bring sight to the eyes
and insight to the mind.
Open our eyes
to the power of your presence,
that our minds may be open
to knowing and doing your will;
now and always.
Amen.

Talking points
❖ our experiences and perceptions of blindness;
❖ the significance of the blind seeing;
❖ seeing Jesus for who he really is.

Activity for younger children
Experiment to find what makes a secure blindfold. Try a tea-towel, a jumper, a hood on backwards and many other things. Use the best blindfold to experience what it would feel like to be blind. Sit in a room with your family, listening to them work, or listening to the television. Try to eat a meal when you cannot see.

This belongs to: . . . .

Make a string telephone

You will need

plastic pots   scissors
string

What to do

1. Find two plastic pots that can be held to your ear or mouth (for example, yoghurt pots).
2. With the scissors or a metal skewer, carefully make a hole in the bottom of each pot. (You may like to ask an adult for help.)
3. Insert one end of a long piece of string through one hole and tie enough knots so that it does not pull through the hole. Insert the other end in the second pot and tie it securely.
4. Give one pot to a friend to hold to his or her ear. Take the other end yourself and walk as far away as the string allows. The string must be pulled tightly. Hold your pot over your mouth and speak into it. Your friend will be able to hear your message. Take turns speaking and listening.

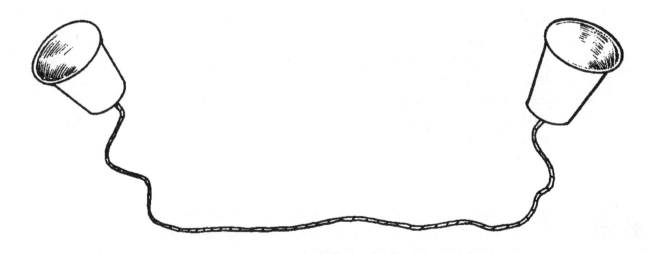

We talk with friends on the telephone.
We talk with God in prayer.

This belongs to: . . . .

Telephone conversation

Today at church
Today at church we talked about how we hold conversations on the telephone - one person talking with another. Then we listened to Jesus' teaching about prayer.

Gospel theme
The parable of the Pharisee and the tax collector portrays two very different understandings of prayer. Jesus commended the approach of the tax collector, not of the Pharisee. No one can stand in the presence of the holy God and feel justified by style of life or piety.

Gospel passage (Luke 18.10-13)
Jesus said, 'Two men went up to the temple to pray,
one a Pharisee and the other a tax-collector.
The Pharisee, standing by himself, was praying thus,
"God, I thank you that I am not like other people:
thieves, rogues, adulterers,
or even like this tax-collector.
I fast twice a week;
I give a tenth of all my income."
But the tax-collector, standing far off,
would not even look up to heaven,
but was beating his breast and saying,
"God, be merciful to me, a sinner!"'

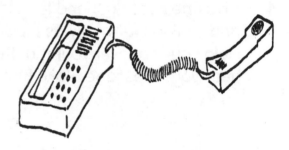

Prayer
Lord Jesus Christ,
you listen to the prayers of your people.
Teach us to pray
with humility and faith,
that we may grow into your likeness;
we make our prayer in your name.
Amen.

Talking points
❖   our experiences of two-way telephone conversations;
❖   prayer as a two-way telephone conversation with God;
❖   conversing with God in prayer.

Activity for younger children
Start your own telephone book with lists of phone numbers for your friends and family. Use a small notebook or make your own book by folding sheets of paper and stapling them together.

This belongs to: . . . .

Make signposts

You will need

card or paper   scissors
pens and pencils

What to do

1. The beatitudes in Matthew 5.1–12 are signposts for the Christian life. Make copies for your own room to remind you of the values in God's kingdom.
2. Cut out several signpost shapes from card. Decorate the edges. On each signpost copy one of the beatitudes. Choose the ones that mean most to you.

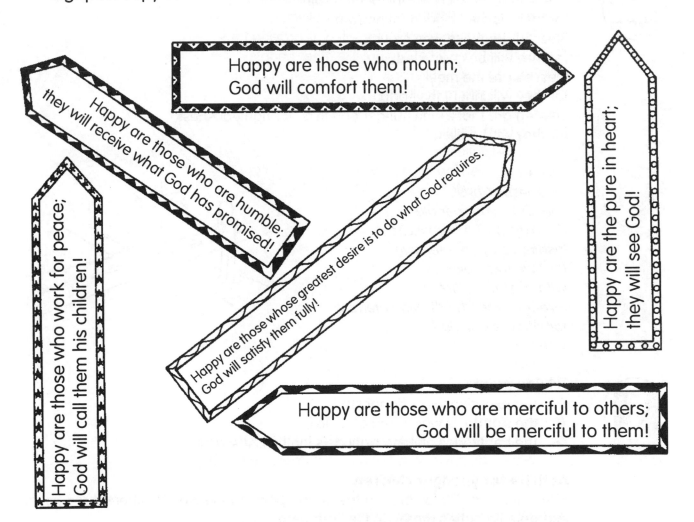

Happy are those who mourn;
God will comfort them!

Happy are those who are humble;
they will receive what God has promised!

Happy are the pure in heart;
they will see God!

Happy are those who work for peace;
God will call them his children!

Happy are those whose greatest desire is to do what God requires;
God will satisfy them fully!

Happy are those who are merciful to others;
God will be merciful to them!

Signposts point the way.
The beatitudes are signposts for the Christian life.

This belongs to: . . . .

Signposts

Today at church
Today at church we talked about how signposts point us in the right direction. Then we listened to some of the signposts Jesus gave to his followers in the Sermon on the Mount.

Gospel theme
The old law was a list of commandments, things to avoid doing. The new law is a list of beatitudes, blessings based on the new way of life. The beatitudes are signposts in God's kingdom.

Gospel passage (Matthew 5.3-6)
Jesus said, 'Blessed are the poor in spirit,
for theirs is the kingdom of heaven.
Blessed are those who mourn,
for they will be comforted.
Blessed are the meek,
for they will inherit the earth.
Blessed are those who hunger and thirst for righteousness,
for they will be filled.'

Prayer
Lord Jesus Christ,
you show your people
the way of true happiness.
Inspire us by your teaching,
that we may rejoice
with all your saints
through time and through eternity;
for you are our God.
Amen.

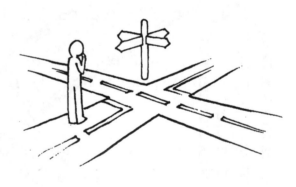

Talking points
❖   our experiences of signposts;
❖   the signposts which God gives to us;
❖   the beatitudes offering signposts for the Christian life.

Activity for younger children
Make signs to display around the house, pointing the way to different rooms, for example 'To Katie's room', 'To the bathroom'.

This belongs to: . . . .

Make a notice

You will need

paper   crêpe paper
craft knife   scissors

What to do

Find out about one person who used to worship in your church but has since left the area or died. This is one of your forebears in the Christian faith. You could get information from a parent or by phoning an older person from church. Prepare a notice about this person to display on the church notice board. Use a heading such as 'On All Saints Day we remember'. Decorate some paper to make your notice attractive. Here are two simple designs for cut-and-thread paper that you can use for this notice and also use later for notepaper.

1. On a sheet of paper cut a set of two vertical lines at the top, just to the left of the centre. Cut another set just to the right of the centre. The cuts should be about 2 cm long. Cut a piece of crêpe paper in a contrasting colour and carefully thread it under the 'bridges'. Fan out the sides to form a bow.

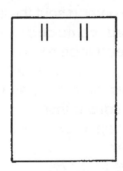 

2. Cut a series of vertical lines across the top of the page. Cut the lines in pairs close together, with about 3 cm between each pair. Cut a strip of paper the same length as the notepaper and the same width as the vertical cuts (2 cm). Cut a second, narrower, strip in a contrasting colour. Carefully thread the strips through the slits.

 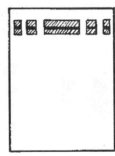

> **We celebrate All Saints Day.**
> **We remember our forebears in the Christian faith.**

This belongs to: . . . .

Forbears

Today at church

Today at church we talked about those who had worshipped in our church in the past. Then we celebrated the festival of All Saints. We gave thanks for all God's people from the past and in the present.

Gospel theme

The story of raising Lazarus from the tomb is a vivid illustration of how we stand and worship alongside those who have gone before us in the faith of Christ. All Saints provides a particular prompt to remember our forebears in the local church.

Gospel passage (John 11.38, 41, 43-44)

Then Jesus, again greatly disturbed, came to the tomb.
It was a cave, and a stone was lying against it.
So they took away the stone.
And Jesus looked upward and said,
'Father, I thank you for having heard me.'
When he had said this, he cried with a loud voice,
'Lazarus, come out!'
The dead man came out,
his hands and feet bound with strips of cloth,
and his face wrapped in a cloth.
Jesus said to them, 'Unbind him, and let him go.'

Prayer

Lord Jesus Christ,
your saints live to praise you for ever.
Inspire us by the example of all your holy people,
that we may follow in their footsteps;
to your praise and glory.
Amen.

Talking points

- ❖ those who worshipped in our local church in the past;
- ❖ our fellowship with those who have gone before us;
- ❖ celebrating the season of All Saints.

Activity for younger children

Visit a graveyard and find a gravestone that interests you. Make a rubbing of this stone, using crayons and paper. Take it home and display it for a week. During the week, remember to pray for that person.

This belongs to: . . . .

Make bunting

You will need

paper or fabric   scissors
string   sticky tape or glue
pens

What to do

1. Find a place in your room where you can hang the finished bunting. Cut a length of string longer than this distance.
2. Choose paper or fabric in a variety of bright colours. Cut large triangles from it.
3. Attach the triangles to the string. Fold the top of each triangle over the string and tape or glue it in place.
4. On the bunting write the words 'I belong in the kingdom of God.'

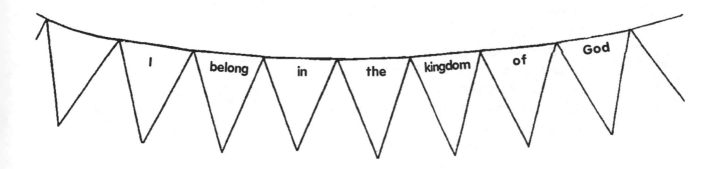

We celebrate All Saints Day
We, too, can be saints of God.

This belongs to: . . . .

Prizes

Today at church
Today at church we talked about the times when we have won prizes. Then we listened to Jesus' teaching about the rewards which God has prepared for the saints.

Gospel theme
The beatitudes affirm the quality of life lived within the kingdom of God. Jesus said, 'Blessed are you who are poor, for yours is the kingdom of God.' Those who live the life of the kingdom are properly celebrated as the saints of God.

Gospel passage (Luke 6.20-23)
Then Jesus looked up at his disciples and said:
'Blessed are you who are poor,
for yours is the kingdom of God.
Blessed are you who are hungry now,
for you will be filled.
Blessed are you who weep now,
for you will laugh.
Blessed are you when people hate you,
and when they exclude you, revile you, and defame you
on account of the Son of Man.
Rejoice on that day and leap for joy,
for surely your reward is great in heaven.'

Prayer
Lord Jesus Christ,
you give to your saints
an unfading crown of glory.
Inspire us by the examples
of your people who have gone before us,
that we may share with them
the joys of your eternal kingdom;
for you are our God.
Amen.

Talking points
❖   our experiences of prizes;
❖   the rewards which God offers;
❖   our fellowship with the saints, the citizens of heaven.

Activity for younger children
Make a display of prizes. Ask every person in the family to bring out any prizes they have won and tell each other about them. Present a prize (such as sweets or a biscuit) to each member of your family for being special to you.

This belongs to: . . . .

Stencil some signs

You will need

card

craft knife

paint or crayons

pencil

paper

What to do

1. Draw simple designs to represent the signs we see in the world around us. The sun is a sign of good weather. Autumn leaves are a sign of the changing season. Butterflies are a sign of new life.

2. Copy the designs onto sheets of card and cut them out using a craft knife. Your signs will be most effective if they contain many small holes rather than one large hole.

3. Use these stencils to create a set of 'sign' note paper to use yourself or to give as a gift. Cut sheets of A4 paper in half to make a suitable size.

4. To stencil the design, hold the stencil card firmly in place on your paper and dab paint over the holes or colour in the design with pencils or crayons, being careful to colour in the same direction for a neat effect.

5. You could stencil the same signs on the back or front left corner of envelopes for a matching set.

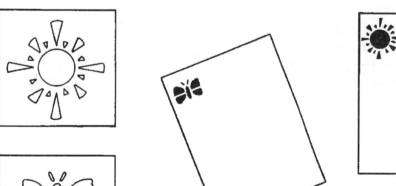

**We take notice of signs in the world around us.
Jesus warned his followers to read signs carefully.**

This belongs to: . . . .

Signs

Today at church
Today at church we talked about all the different kinds of signs we see each day, and about how we read signs. Then we listened to Jesus' warning against misreading signs about the future.

Gospel theme
The disciples ask Jesus what they should look for as a sign of his coming at the end of the age. Jesus warns them against being misled by false signs. Some will claim that wars, earthquakes and famines all point to the end of the age. But Jesus is clear that this is not the case.

Gospel passage (Matthew 24.3-5)
When Jesus was sitting on the Mount of Olives,
the disciples came to him privately, saying,
'Tell us, when will this be,
and what will be the sign of your coming
and of the end of the age?'
Jesus answered them,
'Beware that no one leads you astray.
For many will come in my name, saying,
"I am the Messiah!" and they will lead many astray.'

Prayer
Lord Jesus Christ,
you warned your followers
against being led astray.
Open our eyes to the signs
of your presence all around us,
that we may not be misled
by false teaching;
for you are our God.
Amen.

Talking points
❖   our experiences of signs;
❖   reading signs properly;
❖   Jesus' warning against misreading signs.

Activity for younger children
Make a hanging sculpture to show signs of wind outside. Keep it in the garden for a week. Cut long strips of plastic from a supermarket bag. Tie these onto a long piece of string. Ask an adult to tie the string across a section of the garden, placing it high enough so that no one will walk into the string. The plastic streamers will dance as a sign of wind.

This belongs to: . . . .

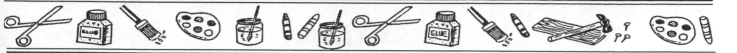

Make chocolate smile biscuits

You will need

120 g butter	120 g sugar
2 drops vanilla essence	1 egg
120 g flour	90 g coconut
1 teaspoon baking powder	2 tablespoons cocoa

What to do

1. Ask an adult to heat the oven to 180°C (350°F or gas mark 4).
2. Mix together and beat the butter, sugar and essence until it is soft and the colour of cream.
3. Beat in the egg and mix in all the dry ingredients.
4. Scoop up a heaped teaspoon of mixture at a time. Roll into small balls and then shape into a smile (crescent). Place the smiles on a baking tray and flatten them with a fork.
5. Bake for 15 to 20 minutes.
6. Eat as they are, or add chocolate icing.

**Smiles are a message of love.
Jesus said we should love God and love our neighbours.**

This belongs to: . . . .

Smiles

Today at church
Today at church we talked about how our faces show our feelings towards other people. When we smile we show friendship and love. Then we listened to the two great commandments - to love God and to love our neighbours.

Gospel theme
The gospels point to the centrality of the two great commandments. The first command is to 'love the Lord your God'. The second command is to 'love your neighbour as yourself'.

Gospel passage (Mark 12.28-31)
One of the scribes asked Jesus,
'Which commandment is the first of all?'
Jesus answered, 'The first is,
"Hear, O Israel: the Lord our God, the Lord is one;
you shall love the Lord your God with all your heart,
and with all your soul, and with all your mind,
and with all your strength."
The second is this,
"You shall love your neighbour as yourself."
There is no other commandment greater than these.'

Prayer
Lord God,
we are created in your image.
Give us grace
to love you with all our heart,
to praise you with all our soul,
to trust you with all our mind,
and to serve you with all our strength,
that we may grow in your likeness;
through Jesus Christ our Lord.
Amen.

Talking points
❖   our experiences of smiles as a message of love;
❖   the importance of love in the gospel;
❖   loving God and our neighbour.

Activity for younger children
Cut out a large paper or cardboard smile. On it glue or draw pictures or write names of people who you love.

This belongs to: . . . .

Stencil some sheep

You will need

cardboard   pencil
craft knife   paper
crayons, pens or paint

What to do

1. Design an outline of a single sheep or of several sheep, or copy the outline below. Make sure your design has many separate parts rather than one big one.

2. Draw your sheep on cardboard. Carefully cut out the shapes with a craft knife.

3. Use this stencil to make a frieze for your wall. A frieze can be a long narrow strip of paper attached around the room. Hold the stencil in place while you colour over the holes, then move the stencil to add more sheep. Make most sheep white but add a few black sheep to see how they stand out from the crowd.

    *   If the frieze paper is coloured, then paint the sheep white and black.
    *   If the frieze paper is white, then draw around the outlines of the white sheep and paint or colour the black sheep completely. If you are using crayons or pencils, you will get a neater effect if you colour in the same direction with every stroke.

**A black sheep stands out from the flock.
Christians stand out for their faith.**

This belongs to: . . . .

Black sheep

Today at church
Today at church we talked about how the black sheep stands out so clearly among a flock of white sheep. Then we heard how Zacchaeus was willing to stand out in a crowd in order to see Jesus.

Gospel theme
Zacchaeus is a man who stands out in the crowd. As a tax collector he would not have been a popular man. Now Zacchaeus runs the risk of standing out in the crowd as one who wishes to see Jesus.

Gospel passage (Luke 19.1–4)
Jesus entered Jericho and was passing through it.
A man was there named Zacchaeus;
he was a chief tax-collector and was rich.
He was trying to see who Jesus was,
but on account of the crowd he could not,
because he was short in stature.
So he ran ahead and climbed a sycamore tree to see Jesus,
because he was going to pass that way.

Prayer
Lord Jesus Christ,
Zacchaeus climbed the tree
to see you better.
Raise our eyes
above the horizon of our world,
that we too may glimpse your presence
and our lives may be changed by your power;
for you are our God.
Amen.

Talking points
- ❖ our experiences of the black sheep;
- ❖ how the Christian stands out as different;
- ❖ standing out for our faith.

Activity for younger children
Draw a sheep on cardboard. Cover it with cotton wool. Colour the wool black with felt tip pens.

This belongs to: . . . .

Make a light switch

You will need

battery   bulb holder with bulb   sticky tape

scissors   2 drawing pins   piece of cork

3 pieces of wire   paperclip

What to do

1. Bare the ends of the pieces of wire. Twist an end of one piece around a drawing pin. Repeat with a second wire and pin. Push the drawing pins into the cork.

2. Tape one wire to the top of the battery. Fix the other wire to the bulb holder.

3. Fix one end of the third wire to the other side of the bulb holder. Fix the opposite end to the bottom of the battery. Test that the circuit is complete by holding a metal object (such as a coin) over the drawing pins. The bulb will light up.

4. To make an on/off switch, fix a paperclip around one drawing pin. Bend the opposite end up so that it does not touch the second pin. The paperclip becomes the switch. When you press it down to touch the pin (completing the circuit) the bulb lights up. When you let it go, the clip springs back and the bulb goes out.

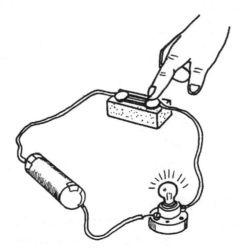

We prepare by checking that our batteries are charged.
We prepare for Jesus' coming during the Advent watch.

This belongs to: . . . .

Batteries

Today at church
Today at church we talked about how our torches, toys and radios need new batteries to keep working. Then we heard Jesus' teaching about the foolish women who forgot to take oil for their lamps.

Gospel theme
Matthew issues the warning 'Watch therefore, for you do not know on what day your Lord is coming.' This warning is then illustrated by the story of the foolish and wise bridesmaids. The wise take spare oil for their lamps and the foolish do not. By the time the bridegroom arrives their lamps have gone out. Like the wise bridesmaids we are exhorted to have enough oil.

Gospel passage (Matthew 25.1-4)
Jesus said, 'The kingdom of heaven will be like this.
Ten bridesmaids took their lamps
and went to meet the bridegroom.
Five of them were foolish, and five were wise.
When the foolish took their lamps, they took no oil with them;
but the wise took flasks of oil with their lamps.'

Prayer
Lord Jesus Christ,
you welcome those
who are prepared for your coming.
Fill our lamps with oil that never runs out,
that our lives may shine
ready for your kingdom;
for you reign for ever.
Amen.

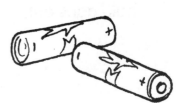

Talking points
❖   our experiences of batteries;
❖   the call to be prepared;
❖   watching for the coming of Christ during Advent.

Activity for younger children
Sort your toys into groups - those which need batteries and those which do not. Try playing with some of the battery toys without switching them on. How well can you play with them if you have not prepared well enough to make sure the batteries work?

This belongs to: . . . .

Make a fishing picture

You will need

net or mesh   paper or card
glue or stapler   scissors
pens or pencils

What to do

1. Find some net or mesh to look like a fishing net. You could use the plastic mesh from bags for selling oranges. Cut out a rectangle of mesh and a rectangle of backing paper or card slightly smaller than the mesh.
2. Draw brightly coloured fish on paper and cut them out.
3. Colour the backing sheet blue/green to look like the sea.
4. Place the fish on the backing sheet. Cover with the mesh to look like fish caught in a net. Glue or staple the edges of the net to the back of the backing sheet.
5. Display in your room.

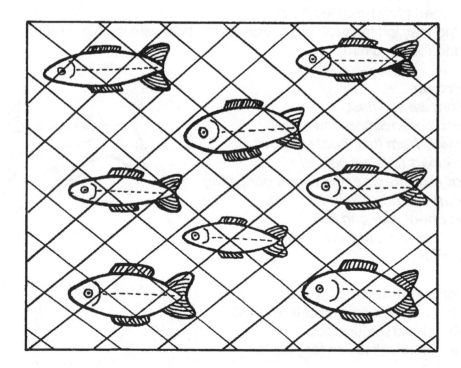

Jesus chose four fishermen as his disciples.
He called them to fish for people.

This belongs to: . . . .

Fishing nets

Today at church
Today at church we talked about how fishing nets are used to catch fish. Then we heard how Jesus' first disciples were fishermen. They left their fishing nets to call people to follow Jesus.

Gospel theme
Saint Mark's gospel begins with Jesus calling the first four disciples, Simon and his brother Andrew, and James and his brother John. All four were fishermen. Called away from their trade as fishermen, Jesus equipped them to fish for people.

Gospel passage (Mark 1.16–20)
As Jesus passed along the Sea of Galilee,
he saw Simon and his brother Andrew casting a net into the lake –
for they were fishermen.
And Jesus said to them,
'Follow me and I will make you fish for people.'
And immediately they left their nets and followed him.
As he went a little farther,
he saw James son of Zebedee and his brother John,
who were in their boat mending the nets.
Immediately he called them;
and they left their father Zebedee in the boat with the hired men,
and followed him.

Prayer
Lord Jesus Christ,
you called Simon and Andrew
away from their boat to follow you.
Help us to leave behind
all that stands in the way of our calling,
that we may follow you
in obedience and love;
for you are our God.
Amen.

Talking points
❖ our experiences of fishing nets;
❖ the first four disciples;
❖ their call to fish for people.

Activity for younger children
Play a fishing game in the bath. Fill the bath with water. Put in toys or small plastic kitchen items that float. Make a fishing net using the plastic mesh from orange bags, or use an old net curtain. See how many 'fish' you can catch in the net.

This belongs to: . . . .

Make butterfly gift cards

You will need

coloured card
scissors
ribbon

pencil
paper gift tie

What to do

1. Cut a piece of coloured card to the size of an opened gift tag. Fold it in half.

    Cut out a butterfly shape from a piece of card in a contrasting colour. Glue it to the front of the gift tag.

    Punch a hole in the top and thread through a length of coloured paper ribbon to attach it to a gift.

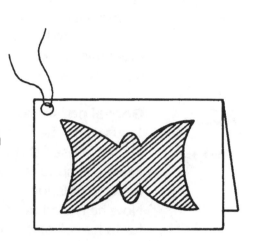

2. Cut a piece of coloured card to a size slightly larger than an opened gift tag. (This size allows for the pieces that will be cut away.) Fold it in half.

    On the front draw the outline of half a butterfly, using up most of the card. Cut out the shape, cutting through both pieces of card so that the shape opens up as a complete butterfly. Decorate it.

    Punch a hole in the top and thread through a length of coloured paper ribbon to attach it to a gift.

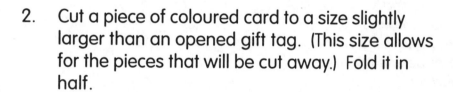
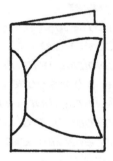

A caterpillar's life is different from a butterfly's. Jesus said the afterlife is different from this one.

This belongs to: . . . .

Butterflies

Today at church
Today at church we talked about how caterpillars turn into beautiful butterflies. Then we listened to Jesus' teaching about eternal life.

Gospel theme
Jesus became embroiled in an established argument between Sadducees and Pharisees regarding the afterlife. The Sadducees try to demonstrate that strict adherence to the Law of Moses makes belief in the afterlife absurd. Jesus indicates that their argument misrepresents the afterlife. The afterlife is of a different order from this life.

Gospel passage (Luke 20.37-38)
Jesus said, 'The fact that the dead are raised
Moses himself showed, in the story about the bush,
where he speaks of the Lord as the God of Abraham,
the God of Isaac, and the God of Jacob.
Now he is God not of the dead, but of the living;
for to him all of them are alive.'

Prayer
Lord Jesus Christ,
to your reign there is no end.
Rejoicing with all your followers
who have gone before us in the way,
we pray that we may be one with them
in your eternal kingdom;
for ever and ever.
Amen.

Talking points
❖ our experiences of caterpillars and butterflies;
❖ how the same life can be expressed in different ways;
❖ seeing the afterlife as different from this life.

Activity for younger children
Put splodges of paint onto a sheet of paper. Fold the paper in half and press firmly across the paper, away from the fold line. Open up the paper to reveal a beautiful butterfly shape.

This belongs to: . . . .

Make a briefcase

You will need

cardboard box   masking tape
scissors or craft knife   paper
pens

What to do

1. You can use a grocery box for this. Put the top flaps in place and seal them with masking tape so the box is completely closed.

2. Cut around the box with a craft knife, cutting off the top 5 cm. This becomes the briefcase lid. Cut around again, cutting off the bottom 7 cm to be the bottom of the briefcase. Join these two pieces together at the back with strips of masking tape as the hinges.

3. Cut a strip of card from the left over pieces to make a handle. This should be about 3 cm wide and 12 cm long. Tape it to the front of the bottom part of the briefcase, bending it so that it sticks out.

4. Paint or decorate the briefcase. Use masking tape to keep it closed, or punch a hole in the top and bottom parts, thread through string and tie it closed.

5. On strips of paper write down all your abilities and interests, one to a piece of paper. Store these inside the briefcase. We are in business for God. How can you use your abilities to serve God?

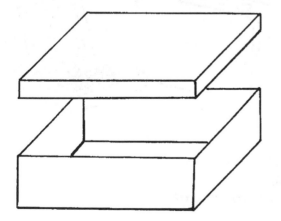
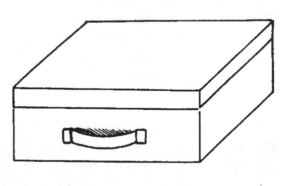

**We have many interests and abilities.
We can use these for God.**

This belongs to: . . . .

In business

Today at church
Today at church we talked about local businesses - offices, shops and factories. Then we listened to Jesus' teaching about making good use of the gifts given to us by God.

Gospel theme
Matthew is concentrating on the theme of the disciples waiting for the Lord's return at the end of the age. The faithful servants were required to be active and to make full use of all that their master had entrusted to them. Waiting for the Lord to come is not a passive but an active commitment.

Gospel passage (Matthew 25.14-18)
Jesus said, 'The kingdom of heaven is as if a man, going on a journey,
summoned his slaves and entrusted his property to them;
to one he gave five talents,
to another two, to another one,
to each according to his ability.
Then he went away.
The one who had received the five talents
went off at once and traded with them,
and made five more talents.
In the same way,
the one who had the two talents made two more talents.
But the one who had received the one talent
went off and dug a hole in the ground
and hid his master's money.'

Prayer
Lord Jesus Christ,
all that we have comes from you.
Teach us so to use
what you have given us,
that our lives may praise your name;
now and always.
Amen.

Talking points
❖ our experiences of local businesses;
❖ why the faithful servant is rewarded;
❖ making good use of all the Lord has entrusted to us.

Activity for younger children
Make a collage picture of local businesses or shops. Visit them to see what is in your local area. Cut out pieces of paper the shape of the buildings, then contrasting pieces for roofs, windows and doors. Write the names of the businesses on the front.

This belongs to: . . . .

Keep a demolition chart

You will need

paper   pen or pencil

What to do

1. Walk around the local area and look for signs of demolition, such as skips full of building rubbish or piles of building materials. Try to work out what is happening.
2. Each week look at these locations again. See what changes have been made. Look for signs of rebuilding. Keep a dated record of changes, like the chart below.

location	date	signs of demolition	signs of rebuilding

Jesus warned that the temple would be demolished.
He promised he would return to earth.

This belongs to: . . . .

Demolition

Today at church
Today at church we talked about how large buildings are demolished to make way for something new. Then we heard Jesus' teaching about how the temple in Jerusalem would be demolished.

Gospel theme
In Mark 13 Jesus prepares the disciples and the church for the last days by emphasising two clear points. On the one hand, Jesus affirms the reality of the last days. On the other hand, Jesus projects this time into the future. The temple will be destroyed, but that in itself will not be a sign that the end is near.

Gospel passage (Mark 13.1-2)
As Jesus came out of the temple,
one of his disciples said to him,
'Look, Teacher, what large stones and what large buildings!'
Then Jesus asked him,
'Do you see these great buildings?
Not one stone will be left here upon another;
all will be thrown down.'

Prayer
Lord Jesus Christ,
all things decay,
but you endure for ever.
Teach us to place our trust
in the things that last,
that we live our lives for you;
for you are our God.
Amen.

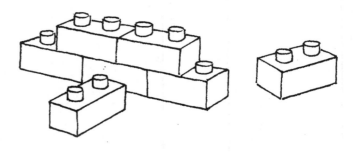

Talking points
❖ our experiences of demolition;
❖ the demolition of the temple;
❖ Jesus' second coming.

Activity for younger children
Build a structure from wooden blocks or other construction material. Use a toy truck as a demolition unit. How many pushes does it take until the whole structure is demolished? It is fun to demolish toy structures but we feel sad when a building we love is demolished.

This belongs to: . . . .

Keep a scrapbook

You will need

book

scissors

glue

pen or pencil

wallpaper or wrapping paper

sticky tape

2 sheets of coloured paper

What to do

1. Buy or make a scrapbook.
2. Cover it with decorative paper such as wallpaper or wrapping paper. To cover the book, lay it open on a sheet of paper larger than the book and cut away the corners of the paper as shown. Fold these corners down into the inside cover and glue or tape them in place. Hide the folded over corners by gluing a sheet of paper over the inside cover.
3. Inside this scrapbook glue newspaper cuttings and pictures about wars in the world. On one page glue a cutting. On the opposite page write a prayer about the news.

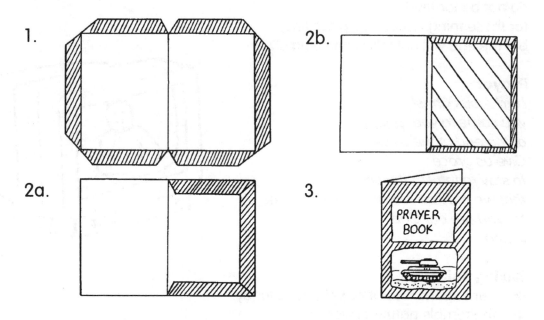

A war is a time of terror.
We look to Jesus in hope.

This belongs to: . . . .

News of wars

Today at church
Today at church we talked about how the television, radio and newspapers report news about wars across the world. Then we listened to Jesus' teaching about the future.

Gospel theme
Throughout the history of the church there have been those who have misread the signs of the times and prophesied the second coming of Christ and the end of the ages. As Jesus prepared for his journey to the cross, he warned his followers against being misled by such claims.

Gospel passage (Luke 21.7-9)
They asked Jesus,
'Teacher, when will this be,
and what will be the sign that this is about to take place?'
And Jesus said,
'Beware that you are not led astray;
for many will come in my name and say,
"I am he!" and, 'The time is near!"
Do not go after them.
When you hear of wars and insurrections,
do not be terrified;
for these things must take place first,
but the end will not follow immediately.'

Prayer
Lord Jesus Christ,
you come to your people
at the end of the ages.
Give us grace
to stay faithful to the end,
that we may be ready for your coming;
for you are our God.
Amen.

Talking points
❖ our experiences of news of wars today;
❖ the terrible nature of wars;
❖ looking faithfully to Christ.

Activity for younger children
Make a prayer poster. Glue on it newspaper pictures and headlines about war. Pray for the people involved.

This belongs to: . . . .

Make a fairground sweet cone

You will need

20 cm square of wrapping paper   gold or silver paper
scissors   glue
tissue paper   sweets

What to do

1. Tilt the square of wrapping paper to face you like a diamond. Roll the paper into a cone with a corner at the bottom, narrow end. Glue the overlapping edges of the cone to hold it in shape.
2. Flatten the closed end of the cone.
3. Cut out a small crown from gold or silver paper. Arrange it around the flattened end of the cone and glue it in place.
4. Partly fill the cone with tissue paper in a matching colour. Fill the rest of the cone with small sweets.

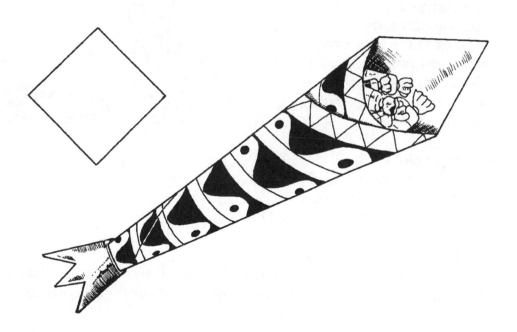

We celebrate at a fairground.
We celebrate Christ as king.

This belongs to: . . . .

Fairground

Today at church
Today at church we talked about our visits to fairgrounds and about the atmosphere of celebration. Then we celebrated the kingship of Christ.

Gospel theme
The last Sunday before Advent celebrates the theme of Christ the king. Here is the triumphal acknowledgement that Christ reigns. The image offered from Matthew's gospel is that of the Son of Man coming in his glory, and all the angels with him.

Gospel passage (Matthew 25.31-33)
Jesus said, 'When the Son of Man comes in his glory,
and all the angels with him,
then he will sit on the throne of his glory.
All the nations will be gathered before him,
and he will separate people one from another
as a shepherd separates the sheep from the goats,
and he will put the sheep at his right hand
and the goats at the left.'

Prayer
Lord Jesus Christ,
you reign for ever.
Help us to see your face
in the needs of those around us,
that we may truly serve you;
for you are the king of glory.
Amen.

Talking points
❖   our experiences of fairgrounds;
❖   the spirit of celebration;
❖   celebrating the kingship of Christ.

Activity for younger children
Cut out a large paper crown from bright paper. Glue it to a flag. Write underneath 'Christ is king!' Display the flag near a window to flutter in the breeze.

This belongs to: . . . .

Make a carnival crown

You will need

coloured card   paper
scissors   glue

What to do

1. Carnival is a time to celebrate with special costumes and hats. Make a crown to wear. If you do not have gold or silver card, use plain card and cover it with cooking foil.
2. Cut out small paper or card crown shapes. Glue these to the crown as decorations and as a reminder that Christ is king over all other kings and queens.

We celebrate at a carnival.
We celebrate Christ as king.

This belongs to: . . . .

Carnival time

Today at church
Today at church we talked about carnivals and about the atmosphere of celebration. Then we celebrated the kingship of Christ.

Gospel theme
The last Sunday before Advent celebrates the theme of Christ the king. Here is the triumphal acknowledgement that Christ reigns. The image offered from John's gospel is from the conversation between Jesus and Pilate. Pilate asks Jesus the direct question 'Are you the king of the Jews?' Jesus takes this as an opportunity to define his kingdom as 'not from this world'.

Gospel passage (John 18.36-37)
Jesus answered,
'My kingdom is not from this world.
If my kingdom were from this world,
my followers would be fighting
to keep me from being handed over to the Jews.
But as it is, my kingdom is not from here.'
Pilate asked him,
'So you are a king?'
Jesus answered,
'You say that I am a king.
For this I was born,
and for this I came into the world,
to testify to the truth.'

Prayer
Lord Jesus Christ,
your kingdom has no end.
Give us grace to be your loyal subjects
that we may honour you in all we do;
for you are the king of glory.
Amen.

Talking points
❖ our experiences of carnivals;
❖ the spirit of celebration;
❖ celebrating the kingship of Christ.

Activity for younger children
Find a long strip of paper. Cut triangles from the top so the paper looks like the points of a crown. Write on it 'Christ is king!' Use this to wrap around your Bible or Bible story book.

This belongs to: . . . .

Make dancing clothes

You will need

paper and card   crêpe paper
scissors   glue or stapler
masking tape

What to do

1. Make dancing wristlets. Cut a band of card to fit around each wrist. Glue or staple long streamers of crêpe paper to the bands. Fasten in place around your wrists with removable tape such as masking tape.
2. Make a dancing headband. Cut a band of card to fit around your head and glue to it crown shapes, or make a crown to fit your head. Glue or staple long streamers of crêpe paper to the band or crown. Fasten the ends of the headband.
3. Prepare a dance of joy to perform for your family, wearing your dancing wristlets and headband.

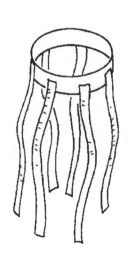

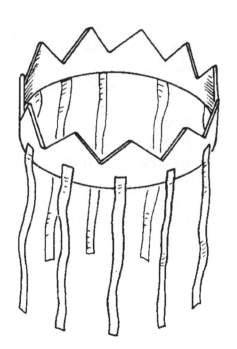

**We celebrate when we dance.
We celebrate Christ as king.**

This belongs to: . . . .

Come dancing

Today at church
Today at church we talked about dancing and about the atmosphere of celebration. Then we celebrated the kingship of Christ.

Gospel theme
The last Sunday before Advent celebrates the theme of Christ the king. Here is the triumphal acknowledgement that Christ reigns. The image offered from Luke's gospel is from the moment of crucifixion. The contrast is between the mocking voice of the soldiers saying 'If you are the king of the Jews, save yourself', and the pleas of the penitent criminal 'Jesus, remember me when you come into your kingdom.'

Gospel passage (Luke 23.39–42)
One of the criminals who were hanged there
kept deriding him and saying,
'Are you not the Messiah?
Save yourself and us!'
But the other rebuked him, saying,
'Do you not fear God,
since you are under the same sentence of condemnation?
And we indeed have been condemned justly,
for we are getting what we deserve for our deeds,
but this man has done nothing wrong.'
Then he said,
'Jesus, remember me when you come into your kingdom.'

Prayer
Lord Jesus Christ,
you reign from the cross of glory.
Remember us
when you come into your kingdom,
that we may live with you for ever;
for you are our king.
Amen.

Talking points
❖ our experiences of dancing;
❖ the spirit of celebration;
❖ celebrating the kingship of Christ.

Activity for younger children
Draw around your feet several times. Cut these shapes out and decorate them. Display them on the wall as dancing feet. We dance for joy because Christ is king!

This belongs to: . . . .